POP GOES THE GOSPEL

John Blanchard

with Peter Anderson & Derek Cleave

EVANGELICAL PRESS

EVANGELICAL PRESS
16/18 High Street, Welwyn, Hertfordshire AL6 9EQ,
England

© Evangelical Press

First published 1983
Second impression 1983
Third impression 1984
Fourth impression 1984

ISBN 0 85234 176 8

Typeset in Great Britain by Inset, Hertford Heath.
Printed by Anchor Brendon Ltd., Tiptree,
Colchester, England.

Contents

Introduction

The use of pop music in evangelism has become a very 'hot potato' in recent years. Everybody has an opinion on the subject. Pop gospel turns some people on; it switches others off. Some see it as a blessing from heaven, others as a curse from hell. Thousands of Christians (mainly young) would travel almost any distance to get to a gospel concert — and would be met by hordes of fellow-Christians (mainly older) trying to get away from it!

There seems no neutrality on the issue. Right across the theological and denominational boards — to say nothing of the age ranges — people are getting very hot under the collar as they argue their particular line. Often the arguments generate more heat than light. Sometimes opponents seem unable to make the important distinction between people and principles, or the equally important one between fact and fiction.

The time has come to take a calm, balanced, thorough and biblical look at the whole subject of what we might call 'entertainment evangelism': *this book is an attempt to do so*. We do not write as experts in any field of music, but we do have a certain amount of access to what the experts have to say and have therefore quoted them left, right and centre. In addition we have access to the Bible, 'the living and enduring word of God' (1 Peter 1:23), and we have tried to bring its commands, warnings, examples and principles to bear on the subject at every stage.

5

Pop gospel is one of the most important issues facing evangelism in Britain today and it has been exhilarating to see how relevant the Bible is to every part of it. Perhaps our greatest rediscovery has been that the Bible is 'the law that gives *freedom*' (James 2:12). To natural ears, that sounds like a contradiction in terms. Law and liberty seem like opposites — but in Christian language they are not. For instance, submission to Scripture sets us free from being tied to *trends*, which swirl around us in all the worlds of the arts, but particularly in music, where the changes can be so sudden. On the other hand, it also sets us free from *tradition*, which can cramp us into one particular culture. It sets us free from *peer group pressure*, the insistence of the majority, which can rob us of the privilege of genuinely free choice. It sets us free from relying on our *emotions*, which are such notoriously unreliable guides as to what is right or wrong. Above all, it sets us free from the subtle tyranny of *self*, the second worst enemy we have.

We are making no great claims for what we have written, but it is our prayer that this little book will help many Christians to set aside their prejudices and preferences, think the whole issue through *biblically* and then act with 'the obedience that comes from faith' (Romans 1:5).

We would like to thank Andrew Anderson, Brian Edwards and Tony Seagar, who read the early draft and made many helpful suggestions. We are also grateful to Mrs Joy Hills for her excellent typing of the finished manuscript.

1.
A slice of history

We live in a world that is being massaged by music. It seems to be everywhere. Background music fills the air in supermarkets and department stores, warehouses, factories, car showrooms, restaurants — even some dentists' waiting rooms! Travel by ship, and it is piped into every room; go by airplane, and it is there, too. Escape all of that, get home and settle down to watch television — it is there again, whether the programme is *Crossroads* or *Coronation Street*, *Grandstand* or *Grange Hill*. Decide to watch nothing except the news, and you are not allowed to see the headlines until you have heard the music. Spin the tuner on your radio and you will discover channels devoted almost entirely to music of one kind or another. Music's penetration into our modern society is nothing short of a phenomenon, something that has a profoundly significant impact on the lives of millions of people around the world.

If this is true of music in general, it is especially true of what is loosely called 'pop music' or 'rock music' — the terms are imprecise as we shall see later — which has such a staggering impact on the lives of young people in particular.

In the beginning . . .?

In his fluent paperback *Summer in the City*, Malcolm Doney says, 'Rock music is not simply another branch

of popular culture. It has shown itself to be perhaps the
most significant art form to emerge this century.'[1]
What is more, he sees its importance as being far greater
than musical; he calls it 'a gauge of the shifts in young
people's attitudes towards sex, authority, taste, their
contemporaries and ethics'.[2]

If these statements are even half true, rock music is
something of great significance that has 'happened'
during the lifetime of everyone in the world under
thirty years of age. But did it just 'happen'? We can
obviously not begin to understand rock music until we
discover something of its beginnings, and, as with so
many things, that is easier said than done.

Having said that, some people find it no problem
whatever: all rock music stems directly from the devil,
and its journey can be traced very simply – from hell
to the African jungle, from the African jungle to
America, and then, on twentieth-century airwaves,
from America to the rest of the world. QED! But that
is neither factual nor fair. Blanket condemnation of the
whole of today's pop scene by condensing its history
into one searing sentence certainly cuts discussion
short, but it hardly helps to arrive at the truth.

The fact is that rock draws from many streams and
is very complex. It is a Mississippi of music, with many
different tributaries flowing into the vast river of sound
we are now hearing, and it is virtually impossible to
trace all of those tributaries back to their sources.

Roots

Even if we do not buy the 'All rock is African jungle
music' line, there can be no serious doubt that the roots
of rock do run back into the West African slave culture
of the fifteenth century, which was eventually taken to

the West Indies and the southern part of what we now know as the United States. Primitive, home-made instruments were later replaced by the clarinet, trumpet, cornet and trombone, with the piano, guitar, banjo, double-bass and drums eventually forming the 'rhythm section'.

Music played a very important role in the lives of the slaves, enabling them to express their emotions in terms of their own traditional culture rather than in those dictated by their grim conditions. Yet eventually they began to assimilate some of the other musical values with which they were surrounded — ballads from Elizabethan England, quadrilles from France, traditional Spanish dances, which were particularly popular in Louisiana, and, of course, the country music that was already becoming 'American' in its own right.

In the development of all art forms, there is a mixture of assimilation and innovation and the same was true in the development of popular music. Slowly, distinctive styles began to emerge and to spread and this continued right through the time of the slaves' emancipation in 1865 and on into the twentieth century itself. Blues (slow and sad), rhythm and blues (more heavily accented), gospel (adaptation of hymn tunes), rag-time (strongly syncopated) and jazz (lots of improvisation) — one trend led to another. Nothing was entirely new; every development of style borrowed something from the past and reflected something of the present, mirroring its moods and expressing them in popular form. Steve Lawhead summarizes it by saying that these developing musical styles 'were formed in the give-and-take of many cultural backgrounds (German, Czech, French, Irish, English and others) over many years'[3] and adds, 'Even the music of Africa did not originate spontaneously on its own. It was shaped by its contact with Europe, Asia and the Middle East.'[4]

Not that dispersing the roots of rock sanctifies it. The original blues singers rejected the Christian faith as part of a hostile white culture, and placed a heavy emphasis on 'the pleasure of this world, particularly the enjoyment of illicit sex . . . Heaven, if it existed, was to be peopled with dancing girls.'[5] Rod Gruver says that the blues poets insisted that 'no other love can compare with the love that comes either before or outside marriage'.[6]

These examples alone serve to remind us of one simple fact — that in *all* cultures we must expect to find an underlying trend of values that are not just sub-Christian but anti-Christian. Man is *fallen*, and his fallenness comes to the surface in every age, in every country and in every part of his culture. It is all part of what the Bible means when it says, 'All have sinned and *fall short* of the glory of God' (Romans 3:23) and our italics emphasize the fact that man's fallenness is a continuing reality.

Haley's Comets

Popular music after the end of World War II was a tired hangover from what went before — romantic, sentimental and *predictable*. But by the early nineteen-fifties the new generation of American teenager was discovering other sounds — updated versions of blues and rhythm and blues, in which 'the vocals were rough and uncompromising, the lyrics personal and explicit'.[7] Primarily, it was black music, but soon white groups began to play it. Leading the way was a middle-aged country and western group called Bill Haley and the Comets. They would hardly have been typecast as revolutionaries, but by the time they had recorded 'Shake, rattle and roll' (toning down the words), 'Crazy, man, crazy' (the first white rock 'n' roll record to hit the charts) and 'Rock around the Clock' (which eventually sold fifteen million as a single) popular music had been catapulted into a new era.

Elvis

What was now needed was the man to match the music, someone young, raw, mean and exciting — and that someone was a one-time choirboy called Elvis Presley. Presley was worshipped by some and hated by others. To his millions of fans he was 'the King', to others he was not far short of the personification of everything evil. He appeared arrogant, sensuous, obscene. He was said to consult with a psychic in Colorado, and to be heavily into drugs. One of his bodyguards claimed that the rock 'n' roll idol's buttocks were 'so punctured with needle marks that there was hardly room left for an injection'.[8] When he died in 1977 at the age of forty-two, 'Elvis the Pelvis' had earned 4.3 billion dollars from a career which remains without parallel in the history of popular music.

The lads from Liverpool

Elvis opened the floodgates for hundreds of imitators and followers in the same, raw, aggressive, sensual style, yet, surprisingly, the vogue did not last very long. By the end of the nineteen-fifties rock 'n' roll was disconnected and no longer dominant, its place on centre stage taken by something much more generally acceptable — folk music. Folk was almost 'thinking man's music' compared to rock 'n' roll. It spoke about serious political issues (it was the perfect vehicle for the protest

songs of people like Joan Baez and the legendary Bob
Dylan). What is more, it was *quieter,* with the acoustic
guitar taking the place of the electric version with its
stacks of speakers to amplify the sound.

But that all changed in 1963 with the arrival of the
Beatles. However tame their music may now sound to
many people, the Fabulous Four hit the music scene like
a runaway bulldozer. Their sound has been described as
'fresh, new and inventive'[9] — but to others it was
outrageous, irreverent and dangerous. What *is* certain is
that it was sensationally popular, leading John Lennon
to make his now legendary statement that the Beatles
were more popular than Jesus Christ. As Malcolm
Doney comments, 'The Beatles became more than
hugely famous, they became *cosmic.*'[10]

The Beatles' brand of music was generally less abra-
sive and raw-edged than was usually the case with rock
'n' roll and they were the major influence in the need to
coin a new phrase that would embrace the widening
range of Beatles-inspired sound. 'Rock' became the
post-Beatle word for all kinds of contemporary popular
music — and serves the same purpose today, even
though that can be misleading at times.

The Stones and other stars

The late sixties saw the rise of the hippie movement,
with the Beatles' Sergeant Pepper's Lonely Hearts
Club Band becoming 'the anthem of the hip culture.'[11]
Then came the gigantic outdoor festivals. Daddy of them
all was Woodstock (New York) which was attended by
500,000 rock fans in August 1969 and has been described as 'three days of dope, sex and music'.[12]

Soon afterwards came Altamont, near San Fran-
cisco, when the hippie dream turned to ashes. Three

fans died of drugs, and one was stabbed and beaten to death in front of stage while the band played on. The band playing on was The Rolling Stones.

The Stones' image was clear, but hardly clean. Nik Cohn says, 'They were mean and nasty . . . and they beat out the toughest, crudest, most offensive noise any English band had ever made.'[13] Derek Jewell agrees: 'They projected the harshest, nastiest, sweaty-sexiest and most pointedly offensive musical image yet to frighten all law-abiding Britons with daughters under twenty-one out of their minds.'[14] Drugs, promiscuity and occultism have all been part of the Stones' package — and their influence has been enormous. Malcolm Doney claims, 'It is difficult to exaggerate the impact of The Rolling Stones. They brought upon themselves more scorn and adult hysteria than any musicians before or since.'[15]

The Stones are still rolling, as are others who shared their heyday — The Who, Led Zeppelin, Alice Cooper. Following them we had punk rock, with the music described by Derek Jewell as 'the latest musical garbage bred by our troubled culture'[16] and the punk rockers as those who loved 'hate, aggression, apathy, lust, alcohol, anarchy'.[17] Yet punk rock never really made it and soon the rock world moved on to the next change . . . and the one after that . . . Yesterday's stars are fading, tomorrow's rising in the sky — and the appetites of those who listen are apparently insatiable. Whatever one's personal opinions on the phenomenon, it seems difficult to disagree with Steve Lawhead when he writes, 'For so long as young people feel repressed and awkward, as long as society can indulge one affluent and self-centred generation after another, as long as there is electricity, there will be rock music.'[18]

2.
Identity crisis

Before trying to link rock music's past with its present use in Christian circles, we ought to ask two specific questions. Firstly, what is rock music? Secondly, what is Christian music? The answer to the first question is about as straightforward as the answer to the question, 'What is an Englishman?'; the answer to the second is rather more difficult!

To begin at the beginning, what do we mean when we use the phrase 'rock music'? After all, there is sweet rock and acid rock, soft rock and hard rock, glam rock and glitter rock, folk rock and punk rock — 'everything from gay rock to God rock'[1] — to say nothing of reggae, heavy metal, new wave, disco, new romantic and jazz funk. No wonder Derek Jewell can write, 'No one has satisfactorily *defined* rock . . . you suggest its properties rather than pin it down firmly.'[2] These days 'rock' is a label which loosely covers the whole range of contemporary popular music. Yet there are certain characteristics basic to what we could almost call 'traditional' rock music. What are they, and how do they relate to the use of rock as an evangelistic vehicle?

On and on and on and on . . .

One of the basic constituents of rock music is constant repetition. Listen to any rock record you choose, and one of its major features will be the constant repetition of

14

chord patterns, beat, a narrow range of notes or a rhythmic figure. Professor Frank Garlock, Chairman of the Music Theory Department at Bob Jones University, tells of spending an entire week listening to 1,000 rock records and discovering that only three had anything approaching a balanced structure. All the rest consisted of the constant repetition of chordal, melodic or rhythmic patterns.

There is obviously no 'law' about the amount of variety that is needed before a piece of music becomes 'legitimate'; the most we can say is that variety is one of the marks of any good music, regardless of style. Some people might say that there is considerable repetition in certain classical music, and this is true. But it is *creative*, with subtle variations woven into it. Is there honestly any comparison between, say, the repetition in a Vivaldi concerto movement and that in Led Zeppelin's 'Whole Lotta Love' (widely considered a classic piece of rock)? Quite apart from the erotic elements and simulated orgasm, 'Whole Lotta Love' has about as much variety of sound as a pneumatic drill.

This insistent repetition immediately raises warning cones about the suitability of rock music in evangelism, because *constant repetition has a hypnotic effect*. Professor William Shafer, a non-Christian sociologist, says, 'What is undeniable about rock is its hypnotic power. It has gripped millions of young people around the world and transformed their lives.'[3] Dr Granville Knight agrees: 'There is no question in my mind about the hypnotic effect of these songs.' So does Dr W. J. Bryan: 'Children are being hypnotized without their knowledge, and that is the really insidious part about these records. The more often the hypnotism is repeated the higher the susceptibility of the subject.' In the course of his specialized study, Andrew Salter has

indicated that rock music is an ideal vehicle for individual or mass hypnosis. [4] Even more telling is this statement by the late Jimi Hendrix, one of the most dynamic
and influential superstars in rock music history: 'Atmo-
spheres are going to come through music, because the
music is a spiritual thing of its own. You can hypno-
tize people with the music and when you get them at
their weakest point you can preach into the subconscious what you want to say.'[5]

This obviously has very serious implications for the
use of rock music in evangelism. Any medium of
presentation that induces any loss of self-control or
awareness and makes the listener unusually susceptible
to whatever suggestions are made by the lyrics is surely
dangerous, and will almost certainly encourage a response that will be largely psychological instead of that
which God requires, that we should worship him 'in
spirit and in truth' (John 4:24).

Drummer's holiday

As with constant repetition, driving beat is an indispensable ingredient of rock. As Bob Larson puts it,
'Whatever harmonic or melodic or verbal sophistication
rock may contain, it would never appeal as it does
without the undergirding of its simple, repetitive,
pounding beat.'[6] As with repetition, rhythm plays a
valid part in all music, but in rock music rhythm is
replaced by a relentless, driving beat. The difference
between this beat and genuine rhythm has been well
put by Igor Stravinsky: 'Rhythm doesn't really exist,
because no rhythmic proportion or relaxation exists.'[7]
Bob Larson says much the same thing: 'Unlike other
forms of music which may reveal melodic inventiveness,
the focus of rock is usually on the beat. It is a

drummer's holiday . . . I have known drummers who have actually had self-induced orgasms after several hours of incessant drumming.'[8]

Even without thinking in terms of such extremes, it must be obvious that excessive beat has real dangers. There is evidence, for instance, to suggest that when the beat overrides the other elements in a song the communication level is significantly changed to one which is primarily physical and often specifically sexual. Rock musician Tom McSloy has no doubts about this: 'To *get* into rock you have to *give* in to it, let it inside, flow with it to the point where it consumes you, and all you can feel or hear or think about is the music.'[9] That is an alarming statement — but it ties in perfectly with some words written by someone who comes at it from a completely different angle, the well-known British preacher, Dr Martyn Lloyd-Jones. In his classic book *Preaching and Preachers* he has a section in which he warns of the dangers of preachers making a direct attack on either the emotions or the will. In it he writes, 'We can become drunk on music — there is no question about that. Music can have the effect of creating an emotional state in which the mind is no longer functioning as it should be, and no longer discriminating. I have known people to sing themselves into a state of intoxication without realizing what they were doing.'[10] We can take it for granted that he was not writing about a rock concert — so the point we are making is not part of an 'anti-rock' diatribe. What we are saying is that the element of relentless beat in rock music increases the danger of a shallow, emotional, unthinking response, made at the wrong level and for the wrong reasons. David Winter openly admits in his book *New Singer, New Song* that 'An incessant beat does erode a sense of responsibility in much the same way as alcohol does . . . You feel in the grip of a relentless stream of sound to which something very basic and primitive in the human nature responds.'[11] Surely this is a highly dangerous thing? To quote Lloyd-Jones again, 'The important point is that we should realize that the effect produced in such a case is not produced by the truth . . .'[12]

Dangerous decibels

As with repetition and beat, no time need be wasted in proving that volume is an important element in rock music, with huge stacks of equipment needed to produce the required amount of amplification. This report by Derek Jewell of a sell-out Albert Hall concert by the British group The Cream (now disbanded but which broke Beatles' attendance records in the United States) tells us the kind of impact that can be made: 'It contained some highly skilled, if perverse, talent — especially the guitarist Eric Clapton. But its Albert Hall show was misconceived, an attempt at a gigantic *tour de force,* with the accent on force. I have never heard louder music. It destroyed itself in sheer decibels. The juggernaut of sound assaulted the stomach as well as being a danger to the ear-drums. It was mind-fragmenting music, involving one in what the pop avant-garde fashionably calls total experience. I don't want total experience in a concert hall . . . I want *musical* experiences . . .'[13]

Volume for volume's sake is one trademark of heavy metal, which arrived in the late sixties with groups like Deep Purple, Black Sabbath and Led Zeppelin. Malcolm Doney describes it as 'horrendous, heavy, mind-deadening music . . . blacksmith music . . . a battering-ram against the senses'.[14] As with repetition and beat, volume can have a 'hypnotic' effect — Doney writes of

audiences who 'were only too willing to let themselves
be pushed along. They offered themselves up to the
music. They went to concerts with the specific intention of being zonked out.'[15]

But *how loud is loud*? Sound level is measured in
decibels. In a paper entitled 'Hearing Acuity in Young
People exposed to Pop Music and other Noise' Drs
David Hanson and Ronald Fearn report that in visits to
over thirty youth clubs they found average rock music
decibel levels of between 84 and 118, with only one
rating falling below 90.[16] At rock concerts, similar
readings are common and can sometimes be in the
120–130 range. There have even been readings of
138 decibels. (As a working comparison, a vacuum
cleaner generates about 80 decibels and a pneumatic
hammer 94.)

Yet even these figures do not tell the whole story.
Decibels increase *logarithmically*, not arithmetically,
which means that an increase of only three decibels
indicates *double* the intensity of sound. The standard
British work on the subject of the effect of noise is
Hearing and Noise in Industry, by Burns and Robinson,
published by Her Majesty's Stationery Office. In it,
they suggest that for an eight-hour working day, the
maximum volume level should be 90 decibels, with
the exposure duration being halved for every increase
of three decibels.[17] This means that at 93 decibels
the recommended maximum exposure should be four
hours; for 96, two hours; for 99 one hour, and so on.
Getting up to rock concert levels, the danger marks
would be as follows: at 111 decibels, 3 minutes
45 seconds; at 120 decibels, 28.12 seconds; and at
129 decibels, 3.51 seconds. At the top recorded level
we have mentioned (138 decibels) it would only be
safe to listen for less than half a second!

With these figures in mind, it is not surprising to

find that exposure to loud rock music has had serious
effects on the hearing of the listeners. An ear, nose and
throat specialist in the United States estimates that
about 40% of students entering university have hearing
defects caused by listening to rock music; twenty-five
years ago, in pre-rock days, the figure was 1%. In a study
carried out on 505 British students in higher education,
Hanson and Fearn discovered that 'statistically significant hearing losses were found in the group that
admitted frequent attendance at pop music entertainment'.[18] Other studies by Ronald Fearn in the course
of his work at Leeds Polytechnic suggested that up to
one million young people in Britain suffered some
degree of hearing loss caused by listening to loud music
and that many have hearing problems normally associated with sixty-five to seventy-year-olds. It is no wonder
that Hanson and Fearn conclude their paper by calling
overloud amplified music 'a widespread hazard'.[19]

It has been suggested to us that loudness in rock
music is a matter of conditioning, but surely this is a
highly dangerous philosophy? Should we allow ourselves to be conditioned by something that is potentially so harmful? Hanson and Fearn have the more
obvious and sensible answer: 'The main requirement
must be the reduction of amplification levels.'[20]

Yet quite apart from the sheer decibel level, there
is another factor associated with volume that calls into
question rock music's suitability as an evangelistic
medium. Two very competent musicians, very much a
part of the Christian pop scene, put it to us like this:
'The major problem of rock music is the noise level.
The words are often inaudible and even if they were
audible the degree of truth in them would be negligible.
The whole scene has become a mess, with very many
people not seeming to know why they are doing what
they are doing.' That is a tragic commentary on the

contemporary Christian music scene, made by people actively involved in it — and its most telling point is the one about the music making the words inaudible.

But in evangelism *the words are vitally important.* The Bible speaks of 'the *word* of truth, the gospel of your salvation' (Ephesians 1:13); it says that the gospel is 'the *word* of life' (Philippians 2:16); and that Christians are born again 'through the *word* of truth' (James 1:18). Then how can the work of evangelism be helped by something which makes its message more difficult to hear? In all the reasoning which we seek to bring to bear on our readers in this study of the use of rock music in evangelism, there is nothing on which we are more definite than this: any method or medium (we need not confine ourselves to rock music) which makes the gospel more difficult to hear, and therefore to be understood, is not serving the cause of evangelism but actually hindering it. The enthusiasm of the performers, the sincerity of their motives and the quality of their work may not be in question, but if at the end of the day the listeners cannot hear the *words* of the gospel then all of those qualities count for nothing.

The Christian music myth

If our analysis of rock music is right, using it in evangelism is spiritually perilous. But is it scripturally *possible*? Is there such a thing as 'Christian rock (or pop) music'? The way to begin answering that question is to ask a much more fundamental one, which is this: is there such a thing as 'Christian music' at all? What do we mean by the phrase? Are we describing the *music*? Take a sheet of music from a 'Christian song' and one from a 'secular song'. Are they essentially different?

Is a B flat in a hymn any different from one in a bawdy rock number? Can you tell a Christian quaver from a non-Christian one? Is it something to do with the *instruments*? Is there such a thing as a godly guitar, a sanctified saxophone or a born again bassoon? Nobody is questioning the point that one can have Christian musicians, but the simple fact of the matter is that *there is no such thing as 'Christian music'*. There are Christians and there is music; there is good music and there is bad music (and that statement has nothing to do with taste, style, culture or the age of the performer or listener); there is music that reflects God's glory and music that does not. We can take it further: there are Christians who write and play bad music, and non-Christians who write and play good music. Music is not 'good' because it is being performed in a religious context, any more than music is 'bad' because it is being performed in a 'secular' context. All these divisions tend to blur the truth. Music must be judged not by its context but by its content. Beautiful flowers can be found in a dusty desert and poisonous plants in a lovely garden.

How do we apply this principle? Man's first and constant duty is to honour his Maker in every area of his life — and that includes the most mundane things: 'So whether you eat or drink or whatever you do, do it all for the glory of God' (1 Corinthians 10:31). Every part of life is to be seen as one in which God can be glorified by our obedience to his revealed will. But this is not limited to 'religious' activities, let alone to evangelism. It is exactly here that so many people go wrong. Here is a musician who becomes a Christian. In no time at all, he is encouraged to get involved in gospel music — because 'the Lord wants you to use your musical gift as a means of reaching other people with the gospel'. But who says so? The Bible certainly doesn't. Nowhere does it tell the Christian that he must use whatever talents or means he has at his disposal as a vehicle for direct evangelism.

Lost property?

It has even been suggested to us that to question the rightness of using any particular kind of music in evangelism is to deny the lordship of Christ over part of his creation — but exactly the opposite is true. We deny his lordship when *we* decide that we can use any means we choose, then bring him in at the next stage and ask his blessing on it. The musician's duty is the same as that of any other Christian — to begin with Scripture and discover exactly what methods and means God has authorized. To imagine that by taking any kind of music (or other art form) and using it in direct evangelism we are somehow 'redeeming' or 'reclaiming' it for God is another popular piece of woolly thinking. According to Scripture, only believers' souls (now) and bodies (eventually) are *redeemed* by the blood of Christ; and God's plan 'to reconcile to himself all things' (Colossians 1:20) is something that he himself will bring to pass in 'a new heaven and a new earth, the home of righteousness' (2 Peter 3:13). The Christian is under no instruction or obligation to reclaim art forms for God as if they were some kind of lost property.

Christians should be active in the arts, including music, but they do not have to drag the gospel into their art to make it biblically legitimate. A musician's first responsibility is to make *good* music, not *gospel* music — and the Lord will be glorified by the honesty, beauty and integrity of his work. As Professor H. R. Rookmaaker so perfectly puts it, 'Art has its own value,'[21] and that value is not tied to evangelism. The Christian artist (musician or other) need not feel trapped or confined to evangelism as a 'spiritual' expression of his art form. He has liberty to use his gift elsewhere.

We shall presumably have to go on using phrases like 'Christian music', but it will help us to keep our thinking straight if we remember that there is really no such thing!

3.
Body language

In a report on the 1982 Greenbelt festival, *The Sunday Telegraph* contrasted Christianity's moral code with what it called 'the "sex 'n' drugs 'n' rock 'n' roll ethic"'.[1] The phrase may have been clumsy, but for many critics of the rock scene it probably said it all. They always knew that rock was rotten to the core, and when the good old *Sunday Telegraph* went on to speak of the apparent absurdity of 20,000 young Christians celebrating 'devil's music'[2] there were no doubt thousands of hearty 'Amens' (or at least 'Hear, hears') echoing around the land. If rock has its lovers, it also has its haters — and neither group has cornered the market on prejudice.

In the next three chapters we will turn from our very brief survey of rock music's history to take a close look at its up-to-date content and characteristics. In doing so we will not be short of information. Publicity is the staple diet of most rock performers, and their opinions, convictions, aims and philosophies are often public property. We can therefore get a great deal of help straight from the musical horses' mouths. It may not make pleasant reading, but it will certainly help to fill in the major pieces in the phenomenal musical jigsaw called rock.

Eros rules — OK?

One of the most persistent allegations about rock music

25

is that it has strong sexual connotations — and it is not difficult to see why. From megastar Jimi Hendrix (who claimed to have slept with 1,000 women) onwards, many of its leading performers have made adultery, fornication, lesbianism, homosexuality or some other form of sexual deviation a way of life. Press reports of their sex lives have now become so common that they scarcely raise the readers' eyebrows. Yet we must be careful not to let this prejudice our views about their music. Sin of every kind is practised by people of every kind. No doubt there are dishonest dustmen, alcoholic accountants, perverted policemen and immoral iron-mongers — but that does not mean that their offences are in any way related to their occupations. Nor are rock performers the only *musicians* to have murky morals — even some of the best-known classical com-posers were decidedly off-key in their private lives. Tchaikovsky was no paragon of virtue, Chopin had a reputation as a womanizer, Mahler was hardly blame-less and Mozart's leisure haunts were not exactly havens of sanctity. As for Wagner, he has been described as 'grossly immoral, selfish, adulterous, arrogant, wildly hedonistic, violently racist and . . . a thief to boot'![3] These few examples will be sufficient to show that we need to be very careful before condemning any kind of artistic expression because of the life-style of those who write or perform it. If we took that line to its logical conclusion we would be living in a cultural desert.

We can go one step further and say that many classi-cal compositions have murder, violence, hatred, greed, immorality or other evils as their themes and should be judged by the same standards as any other musical production. But the point at issue is whether we can single out rock music as having specifically sexual con-notations — and the best place to begin is with the musicians and their performances.

Sex on stage

From Presley's twitching pelvis to the present day, there seems little doubt that sex has played a prominent part in the rock music scene, with the sexual temperature steadily rising. In 1977 *U.S. News and World Report* warned, 'Hot-selling songs with sexually explicit lyrics are moving up the charts, causing widespread concern about the effects on youth across the United States.'[4] Today, trying to document examples of sex on stage and record almost calls for a computer. Here are some, with the performers listed in alphabetical order.

AC/DC (the name is deliberately bisexual) have a song which includes the words: 'Let me put my love into you, babe. Let me cut your cake with my knife.' In another song called 'You shook me all night long', the singer refers to a lover who 'took more than her share, had me fighting for air, working double time on my seduction line'.

David Bowie's bisexuality is such that at one stage he was voted Britain's number three male singer and number one female singer. Much of his material is depraved and vulgar.

Alice Cooper, preacher's son turned rock superstar, made a record called 'School's Out' which came wrapped in disposable ladies panties. His song 'Muscle of Love' praises the pleasures of masturbation, while 'Welcome to my Nightmare' was staged by Alice simulating sex with a corpse.

Grand Funk's music (they sold up to ten million records a year) has been described as 'filled with sexual

suggestion and power'.[5] Their manager is reported as
saying, 'Listen man, what takes place on the stage of a
rock concert doesn't happen spontaneously. It is carefully planned to elicit a sexual response from the
audience,' and to have told the lead guitarist, 'Get out
on stage and rape your guitar. That's what the girls
want to see.'

Jimi Hendrix, the first black rock sex symbol in
American pop music, drew this comment from Lillian
Roxon: 'He does things to his guitar so passionate, so
concentrated and intent that anyone with halfway
decent manners has to look away.'[6]

Jethro Tull's concerts have been described as 'bizarre
and loaded with sexualism'[7] with lead singer Ian
Anderson talking about how his microphone 'has an
erection'.[8]

KISS, who deliberately aim at the twelve to fifteen age
group, and have a comic for nine to eleven-year-olds,
concentrate heavily on sexual abuse and perversion. In
the song 'Sweet Pain' they sing, 'My whip is ever beside
me. Let me teach you love in a new and different way.'
The group has been described by producer Bob Ezrin
as 'symbols of unfettered evil and sensuality'.[9]

Led Zeppelin have a song called 'Trampled under Foot'
in which they refer to a girl's 'transmission' flowing like
hot oil while the singer says he would like to 'pump
some gas'. In 'Whole Lotta Love' they sing, 'I'm gonna
give you every inch of my love,' and the reference is
crude and obvious.

Meat Loaf drew this comment from a teenager in a letter
to *New Musical Express:* 'I have just walked out of a

Meat Loaf concert. I was absolutely disgusted by the way Meat Loaf and the female vocalists were acting. Why didn't they just strip off, get down on the floor and have sex? That's what the audience would have loved.'

Olivia Newton-John made a big hit out of 'Let's get Physical' and drew this comment from the *Daily Express*: 'After the soft rock which came from the sound boxes of sitars and synthesizers during the Seventies . . . suddenly, with a new decade, sex is all around again.'[10]

Pink Floyd's album 'The Wall' was voted by *Rolling Stone* as the No. 1 album of the year; it included the lyrics, 'Oh, I need a dirty woman, Oh, I need a dirty girl!'

Prince rated a feature in *Newsweek* entitled 'The Naughty Prince of Rock,' which said, 'He's a prophet of sexual anarchy: his X-rated act has made him a new-wave cult hero and a huge hit with black ghetto youth . . . Prince's apparent religious belief in salvation through sex makes him unique . . . His current road show is a razzle-dazzle riot of erotic funk.'[11] In a song entitled 'Sexuality' he sings, 'It's the Second Coming, anything goes!'

Queen (another name with sexual hints) made a smash hit with 'We are the Champions' which has been described as 'an anthem of gay liberation'.[12] Lead singer Freddie Mercury, who cranks up the group's bisexual image by wearing mascara, nail varnish and hot pants, admits, 'We want to shock and be outrageous.'[13]

The Rolling Stones' typical presentation has been called

'an orgy of sexual celebration, with Jagger as the head
cheerleader'.[14] Their song 'Sweet Virginia' includes the
line, 'I gave you diamonds, you gave me disease' (a
reference to venereal disease). The cover of their album
'Sticky Fingers' came with a real zip; underneath was a
picture of a thinly covered male crotch.

Rod Stewart sings 'Tonight's the Night' and invites his
angelic virgin lover to spread her wings so that he can
'come inside'. He first hit stardom with 'Maggie May',
which includes the lyrics, 'Oh, mother, what a lover!
You wore me out, wrecked my bed, and in the morning
kicked me in the head.'

Donna Summer, the disco superstar, shot to fame with
a song entitled 'Love to love you Baby' in which she
groaned the title twenty-eight times and simulated the
sounds of twenty-two orgasms. The record made her an
overnight sensation and earned her the title of 'the
First Lady of Lust'. (She has since claimed to have
become a Christian.)

Shakin' Stevens was headlined as 'the New King of
Rock' in the *Daily Mirror.* Reporting on his concert,
the paper said, 'Halfway through the performance the
atmosphere sweats with buttoned-down sexual excitement cascading over the guy on the stage, who does
things with the microphone as sexually explicit as the
law allows.'[15]

The Who drew this comment from Tony Palmer: 'They
have a direct sexual impact. They ask a question —
"Do you want to, or don't you?" And they don't
really give the audience a chance of saying "No". It's
a sort of rape.'[16]

These examples are no more than that and we have

deliberately omitted many more that are too disgusting and revolting to include. To a greater or lesser degree, dozens of other top rock groups and hundreds of minor ones show the same blatantly sexual orientation. But does that prove that rock is nothing more than musical sex?

Fact or fantasy?

One of the dangers arising from the publicity given to rock stars is that we end up believing what we see and hear. But that is about as clever as believing everything claimed by television commercials. The point is well made by Steve Lawhead: 'Since rock musicians are image manipulators, most often what they say and do is calculated for a purpose. Usually that purpose is attention.'[17] He gives Alice Cooper as an example and writes, 'Alice Cooper is fairly well known for his shocking stage performances — such as beheadings, cavorting with live snakes, hangings, surrealistic nightmare sequences. But Vincent Furier (Alice's real name) does not sit around at home wearing torn leotards and grotesque facial makeup. According to numerous interviews, he plays golf, softball, watches television and goes about his life much the same as anyone else. His life off stage is dull compared to what he projects in the spotlight.'[18] Malcolm Doney agrees. He calls Alice Cooper's activities 'the product of a crass commercialism'[19] and says that 'The decadent image of David Bowie and Lou Reed was part of the same game-playing mentality.'[20]

No doubt the illusion is widespread. Elton John once said, 'There is nothing wrong in going to bed with somebody of your own sex. I think people should be very free with sex — they should draw the line at goats.'[21]

Of course it produced widespread publicity — but was it
serious? Separating fact from fantasy in this area is not
easy. Yet this does not make objectionable lyrics,
obscene gestures and deviant sexual claims any more
acceptable, nor does it lessen their impact on the morals
of the listeners.

The filth connection

The mucky picture we have painted would explain why
a leading rock magazine can refer to 'prophylactic
rock'[22] and why Bob Larson can speak of tunes known
in the industry as 'masturbatory rock'.[23] But is that how
the performers see it? It is one thing to act out sexual
fantasies to music, but what is their *philosophy* of rock?
Do they see any connection between rock and sex?
Here, without comment, are the views of over a dozen
of those in the upper reaches of the rock music scene.

Johnny Bristol: 'Sex is where it's at in music . . . and
I like it.'[24]

Glenn Frey of The Eagles: 'I'm in rock music for the sex
and narcotics.'[25]

Debbie Harry, lead singer with Blondie: 'I've always
thought that the main ingredients in rock are sex, really
good stage shows and really sassy music. Sex and sass,
I really think that's where it's at.'[26]

Marty Balin of Jefferson Airplane: 'The stage is our bed
and the audience is our broad. We're not entertaining,
we're making love.'[27]

Mick Jagger: 'You can feel the adrenalin flowing through

your body. It's sort of sexual. I entice my audience. What I do is very much the same as a girl's strip-tease dance.'[28] 'Sometimes, being on stage is better than an orgasm.'[29]

Paul Kantor, of Jefferson Airplane: 'Free dope, free bodies, free music, the day is ours.'[30]

Dave Krebs, manager of Aerosmith: 'When you're in a certain frame of mind, particularly sexually-orientated, there's nothing better than rock 'n' roll, because that's where most of the performers are at.'[31]

Jim Morrison: 'I feel spiritual up there. Think of us as erotic politicians.'[32]

John Oates: 'Rock 'n' roll is 99% sex.'[33]

Richard Oldham, manager of The Rolling Stones: 'Rock music is sex and you have to hit them [teenagers] in the face with it.'[34]

Jimmy Page of Led Zeppelin: 'Rock 'n' roll is sexually —— you music.'[35]

Chris Stein, lead guitarist with Blondie: 'Everybody takes it for granted that rock 'n' roll is synonymous with sex.'[36]

Frank Zappa, superstar of Mothers of Invention fame: 'Rock music is sex. The big beat matches the body's rhythms.'[37]

These comments are more serious than those we quoted a little earlier, as they have less obvious publicity value. They may therefore take us a little closer to the truth —

and what the people concerned are saying is that there is a very definite connection between sex and the music in which they are involved. Have they *all* got it wrong?

What's in a name?

To anyone dropping into today's pop music scene from, say, a hundred years back, even the terminology we use would be totally incomprehensible. How could we possibly explain to them that 'punk' and 'funk' are variations of 'rock'? What would 'rock' mean to them? Even more to the point, what does it mean to us? As we have seen, 'rock' is a post-Beatle refinement of 'rock 'n' roll' — but what does 'rock 'n' roll' *mean*? What has it got to do with a particular musical style? Where did the name come from? How did it get used to describe the music it does?

The phrase itself seems to have been born in the American black ghetto communities at the end of the Second World War, where it was a slang phrase for fornication. As such, it soon found its way into the very earthy rhythm-and-blues songs of the time. In 1951 Alan Freed, a disc jockey in Cleveland, Ohio, was looking for a phrase to describe the growing spill-over of rhythm-and-blues music, which he was beginning to play on his white radio station, a phrase that would capture the spirit of the music and mirror the growing excitement it was generating among young people. The phrase he chose was 'rock 'n' roll'. It has been said that Freed chose the phrase to make the music more acceptable to white listeners. That may well be the case, but that was not why it was originally coined and his choice may have been more significant than he realized. One thing is certain, the sexual connotation remained; the fear of many is that it fits the music too well to be merely coincidental.

Not the last word

The secular press can never be accused of undue bias in favour of biblical standards, nor of being overly prissy about morality in general. It is interesting, therefore, to read the following comments on the subject of sex and rock.

Time magazine once observed that 'In a sense all rock is revolutionary. By its very beat and sound it has always implicitly rejected restraints and has celebrated freedom and sexuality.'[38] *Newsweek's* Robert Hilburn added, 'Disco is a temporary thrill — a night in a bordello.'[39]

Herbert Kretzmer, television critic of the *Daily Mail*, wrote that 'Songs, in short, have become the new pornography. Only the deaf, uncaring or wholly distracted will fail to notice this.' Peggy Chrimes, the *Daily Mirror's* television critic, writing about the tendency to screen rock programmes earlier in the evening, complained, 'It is a ready-made excuse to take the sex out of rock 'n' roll, which is a pity, because that's what it's all about.'[40] The *Daily Mail's* Lynda Lee-Potter wrote an article about the dangerous sexual pressures being brought to bear on young girls, in which she commented, 'The entire pop world is geared to titillating the young, in arousing children to frenzied ecstasy as erotically dressed pop stars scream invitations to sexual behaviour far beyond their audience's years.'[41]

Another *Daily Mail* feature writer, Mary Kenny, followed soon afterwards with an article entitled 'The Slaying of Childhood'. Deploring the premature sexual arousal of the young, she wrote this: 'Thus we have on Channel 4 — where else? — the weekly spectacle of the *Mini Pops*, where seven to ten-year-old children cavort

in front of the cameras in make-up, provocative clothes
and erotic postures. Mothers who place their children
in the show deny that *Mini Pops* is an example of
infantile eroticism — but it is significant that Paul
Raymond, many of whose customers do seek pornography, has seen fit to place advertisements in the *Mini
Pops* commercial break.'[42]

Jazz musician and entertainer George Melly has no
doubts about the sexual impact of certain kinds of
music. In his book *Revolt into Style,* he writes, 'The
effect of a top pop group on an audience of pubescent
girls is clearly masturbatorial.'[43] Later he adds this:
'The pop idol is transformed into a masturbation fantasy object for adolescent girls. The shrieking, squirming audience is in the process of self-induced mass
orgasm. Not all girls are prepared to leave it at fantasy
level. Some are so stimulated that they are prepared to
make do with anyone even tentatively connected with
the group, as many a middle-aged manager or young
band boy will substantiate.'[44]

This particular feature of rock is a nauseating fulfilment of something prophesied as long ago as 1965 by
Jan Berry of *Jan and Dean,* who said, 'The throbbing
beat of rock-and-roll provides a vital sexual release for
its adolescent audience,' and suggested that 'The next
big trend in rock-and-roll will be to relieve the sexual
tensions of the pre-adolescent set.'

All of these statements coincide exactly with those
of the rock musicians we quoted earlier, and many
observers of the social scene have come to the same
conclusion. At the annual Headmasters' Conference,
representing over 200 public schools and held at Oxford
on 22 September 1981, The Rev. Professor Moelwyn
Merchant told his audience, 'I think explicit sex is much
less dangerous than the plugging of pop records that
lower the whole tone of human relationships . . . It is the

disc jockeys and their plugging of debased sensory material and the debasement of images who are the real pornographers.'[45] Viewing things from quite a different angle, television personality David Frost described BBC TV's *Top of the Pops* as 'sex to music, when young people go through the motions of going to bed without actually doing so'.

The argument about the relationship between sex and rock goes on. Even Steve Lawhead (who is by no means 'anti-rock') admits, 'There is more blatant immorality being peddled in popular music now than ever before.'[46] But is rock a cause of today's immoral ethic or just a carrier? Exactly how much blame should it carry? Do we indict it or excuse it? Christians must make up their own minds on the evidence they have, relating that evidence at all times to the clear teaching of Scripture. But there is another important question: can we use rock music without any danger of getting tainted by its immoral associations? Richard Taylor, author of *A Return to Christian Culture,* is in no doubt about the answer: 'We cannot foster an erotic type of music and expect to succeed in avoiding the erosion of standards and ideals. Rock music has a message and it is the message of sexual permissiveness. As music affects your body you instinctively want to put motions to it. So what kind of motions fit rock music? Basically sensual motions. If the message of rock music produces that sort of response, then it is not good music for a Christian.'[47]

Analysing the current British scene, *Buzz* says, 'Even the most vocal supporters of rock and pop would admit that there is much in the scene to disturb any Christian conscience. A *large percentage of pop hits* contain in their lyrics blatantly un-Christian morality, ranging from casual acceptance of sex before marriage to the unspeakably pornographic (witness Haysi Fantayzee on

BBC TV's *Top of the Pops*).'[48] Later in the same article
it speaks of a 'tidal wave of songs celebrating young
lust', of Satanism being an 'in vogue image for heavy
rock bands' and of 'rackfuls of sub-Christian filth available in Britain's high street record shops'.[49]

Yet this is part of the daily diet of many young
Christians, who are not enthusiastic about gospel rock
only, but addicted to pop music in general. Many presumably have no idea of the conflicts that are being
set up, but as Bob Larson comments, 'A mind that
has been infiltrated by lyrical pornography throughout the week cannot easily be remoulded with only a
few hours allotted for Christian instruction on
Sunday.'[50]

The apostle Paul gives the seven-days-a-week solution: '. . . Let us purify ourselves from everything that
contaminates body and spirit, perfecting holiness out
of reverence for God' (2 Corinthians 7:1). Every
Christian has a searching responsibility to apply those
principles to every part of life. For many young
Christians, doing so would call for a transformation in
their musical tastes. It might also call for a bonfire.

4.
Strange fire

A second major reason why its strongest critics allege that rock music is unsuitable for Christian use is that it has close links with the occult. It has been said that 'Any fusion of secular methods with sacred intentions is in danger of becoming a truce with the world.'[1] If rock's connection with the occult can be proved, then its fusion with the Christian faith would be absurd as well as dangerous. It would not merely be a truce with the world but with the *underworld,* and 'What do righteousness and wickedness have in common? Or what fellowship can light have with darkness?' (2 Corinthians 6:14.)

Dark world

The word 'occult' means 'hidden, secret, supernatural', but we must not let those vague words fool us and hide the fact that the occult world is real and menacing. One of Satan's most successful tactics has been to convince people that he does not exist, that he and his agents are just a figment of man's religious imagination. Yet no Christian should fall for that. The Bible teems with references to him, and always as a real and living being. He is brilliantly intelligent, staggeringly powerful; the Bible even goes so far as to call him 'the god of this age' (2 Corinthians 4:4). What is more, he is in vicious and bitter opposition to everything that is good, wholesome, pure and righteous. The very word 'Satan' means 'adversary' or 'opponent', and as Dr Leon Morris says, 'Satan is a malignant reality, always hostile to God and to God's people.'[2]

The Bible is equally clear about the existence of Satan's countless agents, which it refers to as 'demons', 'devils' and 'evil spirits'. We read of them oppressing some people, possessing others. They have the power to bring about physical, mental and spiritual disorder, as well as to cause their victims to be gripped by sin of one kind or another.

One of the greatest powers possessed by Satan and his agents is their ability to appear harmless, benign, or even helpful. The Bible says that there are times when Satan 'masquerades as an angel of light' (2 Corinthians 11:14) – and this must surely be one of the reasons why this dark, sinister world has so much fascination for many people. The Spiritualists' Association of Great Britain speaks of the greatest upsurge of interest in spiritualism since Victorian days. An occult book club has attracted over one million members. Large sections of libraries and bookshops are given over to the subject. There may be as many as 45,000 witches operating in Britain alone. Horoscopes appear in over 1,000 of our newspapers and magazines. Even the BBC has fallen for the craze: *Breakfast Time*, which began on 17 January 1983 as the country's first early morning television programme, included a resident astrologer as part of its menu. No wonder Peter Anderson begins the first chapter of his book *Talk of the Devil* by saying, 'One of the biggest challenges facing the Christian Church today is the fact that thousands of people are interested in the supernatural but rarely, if ever, associate it with the ministry of the church!'[3]

Ignorance iceberg

As one should expect, Satan and his forces have deeply invaded man's social and cultural structures — and music has not been left out.

One of the people with whom we discussed the whole subject of rock music and evangelism is a highly qualified Christian musician who writes, arranges, performs and teaches music from the classics to rock. In a private paper he wrote, 'There is no disputing that satanic and occult connections occur in the rock world . . . this is a spiritual minefield and it is right that you should be concerned that many Christians are ignorant of these matters.' Dave Roberts, writing one of a series of open letters in *Buzz*, warns naive readers, 'I'll bet you aren't aware of all the occultic propaganda in your record collections,'[4] and in the introduction to the feature, *Buzz* admits that 'Vinyl blasphemies sit proudly in the records of many unaware Christians.'[5]

How widespread is the ignorance? We can certainly give many examples from our recent observation and experience. We have seen young Christians wearing T-shirts advertising groups heavily into occultism. A record shop owned by Christians had a large central display promoting Black Sabbath's latest album entitled 'Live Evil'. At an evangelical church we found the youth leader playing 'Bat out of Hell' by Meat Loaf while preparing the church hall for that night's coffee bar; he was amazed when we told him of the group's occultic connections and said that he had been playing the album all afternoon — it was one of his favourites! At another church we had a limited opportunity to speak on rock music and the gospel. As soon as we got back to our 'digs', our host went to his record collection, picked out a fistful of albums and said, 'These will have to go. I had no idea these groups were into the occult.'

We are sure that this is just the tip of an 'ignorance iceberg' and that thousands of young Christians are unknowingly supporting the work of rock musicians whose beliefs and practices they would find frightening and revolting.

Check those decks!

However cautious we may have to be in some other areas of the rock music debate, this at least is one in which we must be clear, definite and decisive. Here, in alphabetical order, is a list of rock musicians whose life-styles or music show occult influence of one kind or another. We make no apology for the length of the list.

AC/DC: A hallmark of their albums is the satanic 'S'. Their album 'Back in Black' has a song entitled 'Hell's Bells', including the words 'Satan's gonna get you'. The cover of the album 'Highway to Hell' shows a member with horns and another wearing a pentagram (a satanic symbol). The title song includes the words, 'I'm on my way to the promised land, I'm on the highway to hell.'

Aerosmith: Their album 'Get your Wings' has on the cover the Winged Globe (an occult symbol made up of a solar disc, the wings of a sparrow hawk, ram's horns and serpents and signifying the omnipresence of the sun god).

Alice Cooper: In a story syndicated in the American national press, he told how (as Vincent Furier) he attended a seance at which a spirit was conjured and promised him and his band world-wide success if he would change his name to that of the spirit (Alice Cooper) and allow the spirit to possess his body. During an appearance on *The Muppet Show*, fun was made of his demon possession.

America: Their song 'God of the Sun' speaks about sun god worship.

Ginger Baker, thought by many to be the top rock drummer in the world: Asked about his emotional feelings when drumming, he replied, 'It happens to us quite often — it feels as though I'm not playing my instrument, something else is playing it and that same thing is playing all three of our instruments' (a reference at that time to The Cream). 'That's what I mean when I say it's frightening sometimes.'[6]

The Beach Boys: Dennis Wilson had links with the notorious Manson family; Mike Love and Al Jardine were into Transcendental Meditation. Bob Larson claims that 'The fame of the Beach Boys was a launching pad for the Maharishi Mahesh Yogi's introduction of TM and occultic mysticism into the mainstream of America.'[7]

Mark Bolan, lead guitarist and song writer for T-Rex: He admits to having spent two of his teenage years living with a black magician in Paris and claims to have learned how to cast spells which accounted for the success of some of the group's records.[8]

The Bee Gees: They have an album called 'Main Course' with a song entitled 'To the Edge of the Universe', based on the name of an evil spirit called Shenandorah. They claim that their album 'Spirits having flown' has references to reincarnation, while at least two members of the group claimed to be into ESP (extra sensory perception). On the *Mike Douglas Show* on American television they claimed that their music was beamed by Satan.

Black Sabbath: The name of the group refers to an occultic ritual and they have been known to introduce their concerts by holding black masses on stage, complete with a nude on an altar sprinkled with chicken blood. Their first album, 'Black Sabbath', pictured a witch on the front. Group member Bill Ward says, 'Satan could be God,'[9] while Geezer, the bass player, claims he is the seventh son of a seventh son, is Lucifer, and can see the devil: 'It's a satanic world.'[10] Lead singer Ozzie Osbourne claims he was compelled to see the film *The Exorcist* twenty-six times[11] and on another occasion said, 'I don't know if I am a medium for some outside force. Whatever it is, frankly, I hope it's not what I think – Satan.'[12] Several members of the group admit to astral projection. Their albums include 'We sold our soul for rock and roll', with the cover featuring the satanic 'S', and 'Sabbath, Bloody Sabbath' with the cover showing a nude satanic ritual emblazoned with the number 666 (the Bible's description of the Antichrist). Included in their promotional paraphernalia is a bumper sticker with the words: 'I am possessed by Black Sabbath.'

Blondie: Hailing the group as 'America's favourite new wave rock band', *Newsweek* reported that lead singer Debbie Harry's act began with a wizard anointing a sarcophagus before Harry was released from it to begin her first song.[13]

David Bowie: In an interview with *Rolling Stone* he said, 'Rock has always been the devil's music. You can't convince me that it isn't. I honestly believe everything that I've said. I believe that rock 'n' roll is dangerous.'[14] At one point in his career it was reported that he drew pentagrams (satanic symbols) on his walls and made hexes (other satanic devices) while burning candles.[15]

Blue Oyster Cult: Their symbol is that of the mythological child-eating god Kronos. All of their albums feature the Satanic Cross (an upside-down question mark in the cross of Christ, questioning the deity of God). The cover of the album 'Agents of Fortune' shows a magician holding tarot cards with the message that he who comes against the power faces death.

Savoy Brown: His album 'Hell Bound Train' pictures a train filled with demons and praises Satan as 'No. 1'.

Deep Purple: The group is said to have recorded at least one album in a seventeenth-century castle supposedly haunted by a demon who is a servant of the Babylonian god Baal.

Doctor John, of the group Tangerine Dream: He is an ordained minister in the Louisiana Church of Witchcraft.

The Eagles: The name comes from the chief spirit in the Indian cosmos,[16] and the group was formed under the occultic influence of Carlos Castaneda. They admit to writing most of their songs while under the influence of the drug peyote. Several of their songs, such as 'Witchy Woman', 'One of these Nights' and 'Good Day in Hell', include satanic or occultic lyrics, One of their songs, 'Undercover Angel', speaks about having sexual intercourse with evil spirits and one of their albums bears the goat's head insignia (an occultic symbol).

Earth, Wind and Fire: The group's name comes from the three major elements in the cosmos. Their song 'Serpentine Fire' speaks of the sinal life entity system found in the Shah Krishna Yogi Meditation Cult. On the American television show *20/20* on 15 January 1981 they were filmed in the home of a member of the group which was full of Eastern gods and occultic symbols. On the programme, they claimed to 'have an interest in Eastern religion, astrology, numerology and the occult'. Lead singer Maurice White believes that he possesses powers from previous incarnations and has the group join hands in a circle before beginning a show, so as to tune in to the force of the 'higher powers'.[17]

Fleetwood Mac: The group had a hit called 'Rhiannon' which was dedicated to a Welsh witch.[18] Most of their music is published by the Welsh Witch Company. Lead singer Stevie Nicks sometimes dedicates songs in a concert to 'all the witches of the world'.

Steve Hackett, guitarist with the group Genesis:[19] He recorded a solo album entitled 'Voyage of the Acolyte' with songs based on his musical interpretation of the tarot cards.

Daryl Hall: An admitted initiate of magic, he claims that his song 'Winged Bull' is dedicated to the ancient Celtic religion.

George Harrison: In his days with The Beatles, Harrison was one of the first to turn their thoughts to the teachings of Maharishi Mahesh Yogi. He subsequently became a devotee of Hinduism and a powerful advertisement for TM. His smash-hit song 'My Sweet Lord' (which was accepted by many Christians) is a song of dedication to the Hindu god Vishnu and contains a chant calling forth the spirits of Krishna Consciousness. His albums include a number of other songs promoting Hinduism.

Heart: The group recorded a song entitled 'Devil Delight' which speaks of the sinister pleasures of a 'dirty demon daughter'. In a radio interview, group members Ann and Nancy Wilson did not deny their reported involvement with the occult.

Jimi Hendrix: Before his death Jimi Hendrix was heavily involved in the demonic supernatural. He wore a medicine shirt from a Hopi reservation and claimed that he had come from an asteroid belt off the coast of Mars. He also claimed to have seen UFOs filling the skies above the Woodstock rock festival.[20] Hindu gods were featured on the cover of his album 'Axis: Bold as Love'. He openly admitted that he had visions and communed with spirits.[21]

Iron Maiden: The title track of their album 'The Number of the Beast' is a song called '666'. Lead singer Bruce Dickinson admitted that during the recording of the album a succession of things went wrong, including an accident involving producer Martin Birch's car which produced a repair bill for £666.56. Dickinson admitted, 'That was just too close for comfort. He was absolutely terrified and the rest of us were very shaken.'[22]

Jefferson Starship: This group recorded Paul Kanter's song 'Your Mind has left your Body' and a later album which contained the song 'Light the Sky on Fire', dedicated to 'the great god Kokoa Kan'.

KISS: One-time drummer Peter Criss is reported as saying, 'I find myself evil. I believe in the devil as much as I believe in God. You can use either one to get things

done.' During their concerts they breathe fire, levitate
their instruments and regurgitate blood. Their album
covers bear the satanic 'S'. Their song 'God of Thunder'
includes the words: 'I gather darkness to please me and
I command you to kneel before the god of thunder
and rock 'n'roll.'

Led Zeppelin: On the inside cover of their album
'House of the Holy' is a picture of a naked man holding
up a child in sacrifice to a mysterious light on the top
of a ruined building. The cover of 'Presence' shows a
strange object which guitarist Jimmy Page says sym-
bolizes the force that enables the group to have such
power over audiences, a power known only as a
'presence'. Page bought a house once belonging to the
infamous British spiritualist, murderer and sexual
pervert Aleister Crowley (who renamed himself 'The
Beast 666')[23] and now runs Equinox, Britain's largest
occult bookshop.

*John McLaughlin, guitar virtuoso of the now disbanded
Mahavishnu Orchestra:* A convert to Hinduism,
McLaughlin is devoted to his guru, Sri Chinmoy. He
claims that 'Through the grace of Sri Chinmoy I have
become more aware of the real presence of the Supreme
Being',[24] and told *Newsweek,* 'When I let the spirit
play me, it's an intense delight.'[25]

Meat Loaf: Their album cover for 'Bat out of Hell'
features a demon and speaks of a mutant motorcyclist
riding out of the pit of hell. The group's leader is
reported as saying, 'When I go on stage, I get
possessed.'[26]

Van Morrison: He claims that he experienced a spiritual
transformation through reading literature on Celtic
witchcraft history and the supernatural.[27]

Moody Blues: Their album 'In Search of the Lost Chord' speaks about a musical chord with supernatural properties. The inside of the album cover has a 'yantra' (the visual equivalent of a mantra in TM). There are also instructions to the listener to stare at the geometric designs while the music is being played, in order to enter an altered state of consciousness. The title of one track on the record is 'OM', a Hindu Sanskrit word used for God, in which he is thought to be embodied in the very word itself.

Nazareth: Their album 'Hair of the Dog' has demonic manifestations on the cover.

Queen: The lyrics of 'Bohemian Rhapsody' include the statement that Beelzebub has a devil set aside for them.

Rainbow: Leader Ritchie Blackmore has been called one of the foremost rock occultists and admits that he regularly holds seances 'to get closer to God'. He also claims that when on stage he indulges in astral-projection, hovering above the concert hall.[28]

The Rolling Stones: Group member Keith Richard once said, 'There are black magicians who think we are acting as unknown agents of Lucifer and others who think we are Lucifer.'[29] *Newsweek* once called Mick Jagger 'the Lucifer of rock, the unholy roller' and spoke of 'his demonic power to affect people'.[30] On the cover of one of their earlier albums 'Their Satanic Majesties Request', the Stones dressed up as male witches. Their song 'Sympathy for the Devil' has become an unofficial anthem for Satanists. Part of their album 'Goat's Head Soup' was recorded at a voodoo ritual and the track includes the screams of

those being possessed by evil spirits. The album cover
design includes a colour picture of a goat's head (a
satanic symbol) floating in a boiling cauldron. One of
the songs is 'Dancing with Mr D' and is about a midnight dance with the devil in a graveyard.

Linda Ronstadt: On the back of her 'Greatest Hits'
album she is seen wearing occultic jewellery.

Rush: Their album 'Caress of Steel' has a cover design
featuring a robed man levitating a pyramid. Most of
their albums have a pentagram on the cover. They
perform in front of a pentagram on stage.

Santana: Group leader Carlos Santana has said, 'I am
the strong and the Supreme is the musician. When I'm
really in tune with the Supreme, my guru and my
instrument, forget it man, 'cause it's totally beyond
anything. That's where I want to be.' Two of the
group's albums portray a lion's head; one is made up
of human faces and the other of serpents, idols and
roses. They have an album entitled 'Abraxas', the name
of a leading demon spirit. Songs on the album include
'Black Magic Woman' and 'Evil Ways'.

Phoebe Snow: She admits to ouija board sessions with
her husband, who claims to have had psychic experiences since he was a teenager. She gives psychic readings and one of her songs, 'My Faith is Blind', is about
parapsychology.[31]

The Strawbs: Their song 'Brave New World' contains a
quotation from Buddha as well as a prayer to Ra, the
Egyptian sun god.

Styx: The group's name comes from the mythological

river that is supposed to run through hell. Their album 'Cornerstone' includes the song 'We've found it'. The reference is to the cornerstone of the Great Pyramid — but the Great Pyramid does not have a cornerstone; that is reserved for the pyramid's deity, Lucifer.

Donna Summer: The disco queen is reported to keep in regular touch with her astrologer and to arrange her concert and travel plans around the configurations of the heavens.[32]

Tangerine Dream: William Friedkin, director of the film *The Exorcist* claims that this group's music inspired his film *The Sorcerer*.

Toyah: She has spoken openly about her occultic experiences as a child.[33]

The Undisputed Truth: One of their albums has a cover showing a demon hanging upside down on the cross of Christ.

Uriah Heep: Their album 'Demons and Wizards' features a variety of occultic songs including 'Traveller in Time', about astral projection. 'The Magician's Birthday' also has reference to the occult.

Utopia: Group leader Tod Rundgren admits to believing in astral projection and reincarnation,[34] and that lyrics for many of their songs are based on Japanese and Egyptian mysticism.[35] Rundgren's album 'Ra' is dedicated to the Egyptian sun god and his guitar is in the shape of an ankh (a symbol of lust and fertility). Stage props for Utopia include a twenty-five-foot gold pyramid.

Venom: The members of the group 'proudly declare that they feel possessed before they go on stage'.[36]

White Witch: One of their album cover designs is in the shape of an ankh. They major in 'white magic' of which Anton LaVey, priest of the First Church of Satan in California said, 'Call it black, call it white, call it what you will. It's all evil and it all gets its power from the source of evil.'

The Who: The leader of this group is Peter Townshend, who follows the teachings of Meher Baba, an Eastern metaphysical guru. Townshend put out a solo album which included a Hindu prayer and declared that 'Baba is Christ'. Tony Palmer says that when they play 'there is a distinct feeling of the presence of evil'.[37]

Stevie Wonder: His album 'Songs in the Key of Life' was released to coincide with his astrological birth-sign Taurus.[38] The album cover for 'Inner Visions' depicts the symbol of astral projection.

Gary Wright: On the album 'Dream Weaver' the title song speaks of an experience of astral projection. His tunes are composed while meditating under a pyramid.[39]

Yes: The group's album 'Tales from Topographic Oceans' contains songs said to reveal the science of God, tantric sexual rituals and reincarnation.

That catalogue is both sickening and frightening and there is no saying how many other bands, singers and musicians may be involved in the occult and whose music may be impregnated with the poison. For *Buzz* blithely to assure its readers that the issue is limited to 'an occasional rock singer . . . dabbling with the occult'[49] is dangerously naive.

In the grooves

In addition to all of this, there is the controversial subject of subliminal messages inserted into recordings, at slow speed, 'super-speed' or by backward masking, a device by which the material is inserted in such a way that it only becomes intelligible when played backwards. The concept is frightening, particularly as there are scientists who claim that subliminal messages (including those inserted by backward masking) can be received, stored, unscrambled and impressed on the mind *without the knowledge of the listener*.

How much back masking goes on? Evidence is not always easy to find (which is hardly surprising, given the facts we already know about groups involved in the occult, for instance) but it would be dangerously wrong to assume that the whole idea was a scare-mongering farce invented by rock-hating fanatics. On the Beatles' 'White Album' there is a track called 'Revolution Number Nine'. Played backwards at the right speed, part of the song has a man's voice repeating the words 'Turn me on, dead man' over and over again. It has been said that the Beatles spent 400 hours recording their smash-hit album 'Sergeant Pepper's Lonely Hearts Club Band', of which 200 hours were given to inserting subliminal material.[41] This album, which became a 'classic', includes a frightening drug-trip song 'Day in the life' and 'Within you, without you', a song on Eastern mysticism.

Black Oak Arkansas have a song 'When Electricity came to Arkansas', during which lead singer Jim Dandy makes an apparently pointless statement; but played

backwards the voice says, 'Satan, Satan, Satan. He is
God, he is God.' Led Zeppelin's 'Stairway to Heaven' is
riddled with occultic philosophy. Played backwards,
there are phrases like 'O he is my prince, Satan, the
one who lit up the night. Lord, you make me shout in
glory to Satan . . . Here's to my sweet Satan.' Reversed
messages on tracks by the Eagles are said to advocate
demonism, drug taking and rebellion against parents.
By slowing down a track by Blue Oyster Cult, the
message is 'These women want to take advantage of
my body — and furthermore our Father is not in
heaven'. Subliminal words in a song by Pink Floyd are
said to include, 'The Lord is my shepherd. I shall not
want. He maketh me to hang on hooks and high places.
He converteth me to lamb cutlets. Have you heard the
news? The dogs are dead' (with 'dogs' as a pseudonym
for God). Queen's song 'Another One bites the Dust'
is said to have the reversed message: 'Start to smoke
marijuana.'

How many other groups are involved? A converted
rock record producer said that he knew of fifteen groups
in and around the top forty in the United States who
were involved in backward masking, some employing
witches to insert messages worshipping Satan, others
using satanic chants and seances.[42] An American radio
station 'Brainstorm' reported that some of the most
popular albums have subliminal messages of one kind
or another. What are we to make of this? What proportion of the vast pop music output is affected? What
hard evidence is there that the messages get through?
To be fair, these must in part remain open questions.
Wild exaggeration would obviously be foolish — but so
would a casual 'there's nothing in it' attitude. Satan is
not called 'the god of this age' (2 Corinthians 4:4) for
nothing, and to limit his power and subtlety to what
we think is either possible or likely is to play right

into his hands. Hysteria may not be the right response to the subliminal issue — but neither is apathy.

Under the influence

Many of the quotations in this chapter refer to the personal beliefs and feelings of rock performers. Here are some other statements that speak even more directly to the question of whether the music of those concerned is directly under the influence of occultic powers. Frank Zappa once boasted, 'I am the devil's advocate.'[43] Jim Steinman, song writer for Meat Loaf, once said, 'I have always been fascinated by the supernatural and always felt rock was *the perfect idiom* for it.'[44] Singer David Bowie admits, 'Rock 'n' roll will destroy you. It lets in lower elements and shadows. *Rock has always been the devil's music.*'[45] Mick Jones of The Clash adds, 'There's definitely some inner magic circle with rock 'n' roll. We've encountered it enough times to be certain of that.'[46] These statements, coming from the heart of the modern rock scene, are very explicit. But perhaps even more significant is this comment from Bob Larson, rock singer turned evangelist, from whose works we have already quoted: 'As a minister I know now what it is like to feel the unction of the Holy Spirit. As a rock musician, I knew what it meant to feel the counterfeit anointing of Satan.'[47] What makes Larson's statement so significant is that unlike the many musicians we have examined, he was never 'into' the occult world. He speaks of the 'anointing of Satan' not in the context of his interest in the occult (which was non-existent) but in the context of his immersion in rock music. Is there nothing to be learned from that?

Of course, there are those involved in the production

and marketing of 'Christian' rock music who will suggest
that this smacks of a 'holier-than-thou' witch-hunt and
that secular observers don't see things that way. But
that is not the case. Even as this book was on its way to
the publisher, *Time* ran a feature on Jerry Lee Lewis, a
major rock 'n' roll star in the early nineteen-sixties,
who has just released a 209-song collection on twelve
albums to celebrate his years at the top of the tree.
After documenting Lewis's problems with alcohol,
drugs, miscellaneous creditors and several ex-wives,
Time reporter Jay Cocks quotes Lewis as saying,
'You've got to walk and talk with God to go to heaven
. . . I have the devil in me!'[48] The report then ends
with this comment: 'Indeed, periodically seized by
remorse over a mis-spent life, Lewis will still ruminate
over making a stand for God. But the devil – the music,
and the life that goes with it – always wins out. Shared
or not, that fundamental faith gives Jerry Lee's music,
even to a heathen, the unique power of sin. No smart
talk or side-stepping for him. This is the devil's music,
and Jerry Lee Lewis plays it with the aplomb of a peer.
He may smell damnation himself, but that unholy gift
of his has surely secured him a place in rock 'n' roll's
heaven. Right up there in the dark. At the end of the
road.'[49]

But musicians under satanic influence will almost
inevitably result in listeners coming under the same
influence. Bob Larson says elsewhere, 'It is possible
that any person who has danced for substantial lengths
of time to rock music may have come under the oppres-
sive, obsessive or possessive influence of demons.'[50]
For 'danced' read 'listened', and you have the potential
for even greater physical, mental, spiritual and moral
disaster.

Let us give just one illustration of what we mean. We
have personal knowledge of a girl in whose room solid

objects were moved around by an unseen force. Looking into the dressing table mirror, she saw frightening apparitions. The atmosphere in the room was so terrifying that even her pet dog would not enter it. Pinned to the inside of the door to her room was the sleeve of a rock record by the group 999, but it had been placed on the door upside down, so that it read '666'. In the absence of other known factors, it was assumed that this was the connection with the abnormal happenings in the room. As soon as the record sleeve was taken down and destroyed, the atmosphere in the room returned to normal, the apparitions ceased — and even the dog came happily back into the room.

This is just one small glimpse of the frightening power that can be unleashed even through seemingly innocuous objects connected with the occult. Yet *Buzz* can calmly assure its readers that 'To teach that to be in the same room as a Led Zeppelin record is to leave oneself open to demon possession is unscriptural nonsense'![51]

Put out that fire!

We entitled this chapter 'Strange fire'. The phrase comes from the Old Testament, where we read that Aaron's sons Nadab and Abihu 'offered *strange fire* before the Lord, which the Lord had not commanded them' (Leviticus 10:1 NASB). The meaning of the words is not given, but in the New International Version they are translated 'unauthorized fire', and that helps us to get a clearer picture. God had given very specific instructions about the preparation and offering of sacrifices. Certain things were taboo; precise rules had to govern what they did. But Nadab and Abihu ignored God's commands and 'did their own thing'. The result was

disastrous; we read that moments later 'fire came out
from the presence of the Lord and consumed them,
and they died before the Lord' (Leviticus 10:2).

The severity of the punishment shows the seriousness of their sin — and is a clear warning to us today,
not least in this area of rock music. But along with the
warning the Bible gives us an equally clear command:
'For you were once darkness, but now you are light in
the Lord. Live as children of light (for the fruit of the
light consists in all goodness, righteousness and truth)
and find out what pleases the Lord. Have nothing to
do with the fruitless deeds of darkness, but rather
expose them' (Ephesians 5:8–11).

Putting the negative warning and the positive command together, our message to the Christian rock music
fan as far as any of the musicians we have mentioned in
this chapter are concerned is clear and simple: *put out
the fire*! Demonstrate once and for all your allegiance
to Christ and your opposition to Satan by clearing these
musicians' material out of your life and out of your
home — records, tapes, books, magazines, posters,
clothing, badges — *everything*. God certainly intends you
to have music in your life but 'What harmony is there
between Christ and Belial?' (2 Corinthians 6:15.)

Dave Roberts adds this good advice: 'If you are
serious about being a disciple of Christ you should not
lay yourself open to possible demonic influence through
these records. You should destroy them and discontinue
buying material of that nature. Do not trot out pathetic
excuses about not listening to the words either. If you
don't think about what you are listening to then you
will find your subconscious mind is slowly poisoned
by these celebrations of lust and the occult.'⁵² This
last comment ties in exactly with the warning given by
Bob Larson: 'Whether or not a person listening to an
occult-rock song is consciously listening to the words

really makes no difference. The subconscious mind, the seat of the soul, is being affected.'[53]

What about material from other groups? You could certainly begin by checking the words, the sounds and the album covers. Closer examination might tell you a lot more than you realized! And if in doubt, *never give the benefit of that doubt to the devil* !

Of course, throwing out occult or doubtful material will not be an automatic passport to holiness. The Bible has a story in Matthew 12 about an evil spirit leaving a man, but returning later to repossess him with seven spirits worse than itself, because although the man's house was swept clean it was 'unoccupied' (Matthew 12:44). Make sure that evil is replaced by good. That could mean better music — music that is glorifying to God. On the other hand it might mean a different use of your time!

5.
Danger signals

In the last two chapters we have looked at the more sinister elements associated with rock music, though it could be argued that these flow into the music rather than out of it. Nobody seriously suggests that sexual aberration or occultism are *parts* of the music. Having said that, the connection is clear and close and there is no doubt that rock music is a powerful communicator of their damaging philosophies.

But that is by no means the end of the story. Rock music must by now have been blamed for almost every evil under the sun, from atheism to the crime rate. We suspect that someone, somewhere might be on the verge of blaming it for bad weather or crop failure! Perhaps it is not too surprising that rock gets a lot of 'flak'. After all, it has kept some pretty grubby company over the years.

Pills and needles

Drug abuse is an obvious example. Much of this can be traced to the rise of the hippie movement in the nineteen-sixties. Many of the pop songs which became all the rage then encouraged young people to get turned on to drugs, while others included drug-related lyrics without comment — and the lead came from the top. The Beatles' record-breaking album 'Sergeant Pepper's Lonely Hearts Club Band' was described by *Time* magazine as 'drenched in drugs'.[1]

One of the songs on the album, 'Magical Mystery Tour' invited the listeners, 'Roll up your sleeve, roll up your sleeve, the magical mystery tour is coming to take you away.' In 'Rainy Day Woman', Bob Dylan advocated 'getting stoned', while his song 'Mr Tambourine Man' has been called 'the best of the drugs songs'.[2] By the end of the decade the Le Dain Commission (Canada), appointed by the government to study the drug problem, reported, 'The pop music industry has played a major role in encouraging drug use in general and marijuana in particular.'[3] Addressing the second Annual International Music Conference, Paul G. Marshall, spokesman for a major record industry advertising company, said, 'Record companies and music publishers have earned many millions of dollars from records extolling the virtues of drugs.'

During the Vietnam War, the United States Government wanted to send a top rock group to entertain the troops, but had possible groups screened first to ensure that they were clear of drugs. The plan had to be abandoned because a 'clean' group could not be found.

Not much seems to have changed. In 1979 a leading rock group manager stated, 'No matter what anyone tells you, drugs will always be a part of the rock scene,'[4] while in the same magazine rock critic Robert Forbes added, 'Drugs are a necessary ingredient for many rock musicians.'[5] The Rolling Stones are among a number of groups still pushing drug songs, with 'Brown Sugar' (S.E. Asian cocaine), 'Sweet Sister Morphine' and 'Cousin Cocaine' as examples. Among those openly admitting to taking drugs are Mick Jagger, The Bee Gees, Jerry Garcia, the Doobie Brothers, Glenn Frey, Linda Rondstadt and Gregg Allman; how many others do is anybody's guess. There is a tragic list of those who have died as the result of drugs; with Jimi Hendrix, Janis Joplin, Jim Morrison, Al Wilson (Canned Heat),

Gram Parsons and Gary Thain (Uriah Heep), Vinnie
Taylor (Sha Na Na), Keith Moon (The Who), Tommy
Bolin (Deep Purple), Robbie McIntosh (Average White
Band), Sid Vicious (Sex Pistols) and Lowell George
(Little Feat) among them.

In March 1983 Customs and Excise officials in
Britain reported that heroin seized by them in the previous twelve months had a street value of £59 million
(an increase of 178% over the previous year's figure)
and that drugs of various kinds were being smuggled
into Britain at a street value rate of £1,500,000 *per
day*. Not surprisingly, one university student told us
that drugs were 'as easy to get as coffee'. How drugs
and music merge is unclear, but there are alarming
stories of the result. Jean Alison told *Readers Digest*
the story of her son's LSD trips being set off again by
'one of the tunes he had been singing'.[6] Even more
alarmingly, *Young Life* reported that a young man,
converted to Christ ten years previously and miracu-
lously healed of hard drug addiction, went to Greenbelt
in 1981 and started hallucinating for the first time
since he became a Christian as soon as he got there![7]
Can we just dismiss that out of hand? What we can be
sure about is that anything that might help to create
that kind of syndrome should be avoided like the
plague.

Give a dog a bad name

Other elements have helped to give rock a bad name,
too. *Violence* is one of these and not just when Alice
Cooper splits open live chickens and throws their intes-
tines over the audience. Groups like The Cream produced 'a sort of subliminal violence with which their
audience could involve themselves'.[8] Ted Nugent,

who calls his music 'combat rock' (and wears earplugs
while performing it), speaks of raping his audience.[9]
Mick Jagger of The Rolling Stones is reported as saying, 'Ours is a group with built-in hate. We communicate aggression and frustration to an audience,
musically and visually.' There is a mindless brutality
about heavy metal and the like and no Christian should
have anything to do with it.

Rebellion has been another of rock's companions.
Interviewed on BBC 2's *Riverside* programme on 22
February 1982, Alice Cooper said, 'I've been designing
the new Alice.' When asked, 'What is the new Alice?'
he replied, 'I'm glad to say the new Alice is much more
vicious than the old one . . . the new Alice is the kind
of person you won't want to mess with . . . The whole
idea behind the thing for me is a rebellion. The worst
thing in the world for me is that authority thing. I see
red when I see that.' Alice Cooper is not alone: a great
deal of rock music speaks of rebellion of one kind or
another, not merely against specific aspects of our
society, but against authority in general. George Melly
even suggests that 'A pop movement is attractive precisely because it proposed a revolt.'[10] Speaking on a
BBC Radio 4 programme *Crooning Buffoons*, Ray
Gosling went even further: 'Rock 'n' roll is a beast.
Well-intentioned people thought you could pick it
up and cuddle it. They forgot it had claws . . . Next
time you pass a record shop window . . . look at the
names of the bands — The Slits, The Damned, Bad
Manners, The Vibrators, The Stranglers and Meat Loaf.
The march of the Mods in 1964 was no twentieth-
century version of the Durham Miners' Gala. It was
sawdust Caesars putting the boot in . . . nasty as a
boil, every one of them. I know, because I was one of
them. Behind every sweet doowop and bebop is an
unfettered sexuality and sympathy for the devil:

a violently anarchic —— in the face of all harmony, peace and progress. People could see that when it first happened and it hasn't changed. Anybody with a penn'orth of grey matter could see it was trouble.'[11] The Bible's teaching is exactly the opposite and says that 'Everyone must submit himself to the governing authorities, for there is no authority except that which God has established. The authorities that exist have been established by God. Consequently, he who rebels against the authority is rebelling against what God has instituted, and those who do so will bring judgement on themselves' (Romans 13:1, 2). Incidentally, this points indirectly to the dangers of the popular fad of speaking about a 'Jesus revolution'. Rather than thinking in terms of any kind of revolt, Christians should concentrate on their responsibility to be 'blameless and pure, children of God without fault in a crooked and depraved generation' (Philippians 2:15).

In God's name

Another element in rock music is widespread *blasphemy*. As long ago as 1964 the Beatles' press officer Derek Taylor said, 'It's as if they'd founded a new religion. They're completely anti-Christ. I mean I'm anti-Christ as well, but they're so anti-Christ they shock me, which is not an easy thing.'[12] In John Lennon's book *A Spaniard in the Works* he refers to Christ as a 'garlic eating, stinking, little yellow greasy fascist bastard Catholic Spaniard'.[13] David Bowie sank even lower and once stated, 'Jesus Christ was a strange boy himself.'[14] Others are equally blasphemous and anti-Christian in their beliefs, their behaviour and their music, but have found ways of expressing their philosophies more subtly. John Lennon made this clear shortly before he died: 'Rock music has got the same message as before. It is anti-religious, anti-nationalistic and anti-morality. But now I understand what you have to do. You have to put the message across with a little honey on it.'

Blasphemy became the state of the art with the two hugely popular musicals, *Godspell* and *Jesus Christ Superstar.* The script of *Godspell* is partly paraphrased from the words of Matthew's Gospel, and was hailed by many Christians as an exciting breakthrough in communicating the gospel to the masses — a marvellous way to get the name of Jesus out to millions of people who would seldom if ever darken the doors of a church. Even the now defunct Christian magazine *Crusade* wrote approvingly of it. But the musical's author Stephen Schwartz said, 'I wrote it because Christianity is the biggest myth there is around and I'm going to show what a myth it is by making a joke out of it.' One of the ways in which Schwartz did this was by dressing the characters as clowns and then having them parody Scripture, such as when John the Baptist baptized Jesus with a sponge, making sure to clean behind the ears.

Jesus Christ Superstar, which became the biggest money-making musical in history, also received an enthusiastic reception from many Christians — yet it was financed by Robert Stigwood, a homosexual rock promoter, and written by Timothy Rice and Andrew Lloyd Webber, both of whom admitted to being atheists at the time. Interviewed on an American radio station, Rice said, 'Basically, the idea of the whole opera is to have Christ seen through the eyes of Judas, Christ as man and not as God, and the fact that Christ himself is just as mixed up and unaware of what he is as Judas is.' On another occasion he said, 'It happens that we don't see Christ as God, but simply the right man at the right time in the right place.'[15] Those are very significant

statements. They show that Bible words were being
used, *but were conveying something less than biblical
truth.* The tragedy is that multitudes of Christians fell
for it. The secular press was not always so gullible,
with the film critic of *Newsweek* making this comment
on the film version: 'It is one of the two fiascos of
modern cinema. It has fatal foolishness everywhere . . .
We danced and sang and Jesus was crucified and a good
time was had by all. Lord, forgive them. They know not
what they are doing.'[16] Yet the very fact that these
two musicals were generally so popular among non-
Christians should have warned believers of their dangers.
As Bob Larson says, 'Any time the world begins to sing
about Jesus, Christians should beware . . . The world
hates Christ as much as it did when the multitudes
crucified him.'[17]

The two superhits are now part of modern musical
folklore, yet in some measure they paved the way for
a situation now so bad that Graham Cray can say of
rock music in general that *'Most of it* is used as a
vehicle for anti-Christian propaganda.'[18] The Christian's
response should be obvious. No amount of liking the
music gives him warrant to surround himself with music
whose philosophies and values are in blasphemous
opposition to the one who alone is 'King of kings and
Lord of lords' (Revelation 19:16).

Body blows

There are further danger signals when we turn to take a
closer look at some of the potential effects of rock
music on the lives of those who listen to it and the first
of these warns us that rock music can be *physically
damaging.* We touched on this in an earlier chapter when
we looked at loud amplification as one of the essential

elements in rock — and we can take our cue from there. Articles in the secular press continue to make the point: writing in the *Leicester Mercury* under the headline 'Will the sound of music drive us mad?' Charles Fraser said, 'Irate parents have suspected it for years and now medical authorities are coming to the same conclusion . . . deafening rock music can drive you mad.'[19] A leading educationalist Dr D. M. Beaumont asks, 'Why have music that can lead to hysteria and in the long term to schizophrenia?'[20] At an international conference on noise pollution, a World Health Authority expert testified that loud rock music could cause deafness, psychiatric problems and even temporary insanity.[21]

There is certainly no questioning the physical assault mounted by some forms of rock, such as heavy metal. As Bob Larson says, 'Rock, at least in its harsher forms, doesn't tickle your ears. It jams you in the skull like a freight train. You don't *listen* to loud rock; it baptizes you with a liturgy of sex, drugs, perversion and the occult.'[22] Writing in *Buzz*, Dave Roberts agrees: 'Heavy rock is body music designed to bypass your brain and with an unrelenting brutality induce a frenzied state amongst the audience.'[23] In the same article he says that heavy metal, punk and disco attempt to dominate and master the hearer.[24]

That last point is important. For many performers the avalanche of decibels is a deliberate and important part of their total intention. It is *meant* to blast the emotions and the mind — not to reflect truth, honesty, integrity or beauty, nor to encourage a discerning response or produce any beneficial result. When David Porter says of rock music that 'It is primarily a physical thing,'[25] he hits the nail on the head. So does Mick Farren when he says, 'Rock music is not something you understand, it is something you feel with your body and you know.'[26] In an article in *Reader's Digest* entitled

'We're poisoning ourselves with sound', James Stewart-Gordon detailed some of the serious effects of noise on the human body. One of his conclusions was that 'Noise is most damaging when it is loud, meaningless, irregular and unpredictable'[27] an unintentional but accurate description of a great deal of today's rock music. There are hidden dangers, too. Equipment used by today's rock groups delivers sound at both infrasonic and ultrasonic levels (below and above the hearing range) and scientists are becoming increasingly disturbed by the potential threat to health that this poses.[28]

The sounds of music

There are other even less obvious dangers associated with certain sounds. Timothy Leary, the psychologist who began the nineteen-sixties as a Harvard professor and ended the decade as a drop-out serving a Californian jail sentence for the possession of marijuana, claimed evidence that music of a certain kind had effects similar to those produced by toxic drugs. Adrenalin secretions generated by over-stimulated glands led, he claimed, to imbalanced and harmful physical reactions. More recently, others have confirmed this. David Noebel says, 'Under rock music, the secretion of hormones is more pronounced . . . which causes an abnormal imbalance in the body's system, lowers the blood sugar and calcium levels and impairs judgement.'[29] Noebel also cites medical evidence that 'The low frequency vibrations of the bass guitar, along with the driving beat of the drum, affect the cerebrospinal fluid, which in turn affects the pituitary gland, which in turn directs the secretions of hormones in the body.'[30] Even more remarkable is this statement by Cyril Scott: 'Our researches have proved to us that not only the emotional content but *the essence of the actual musical form* tends to reproduce itself in human conduct.'[31]

We are not left guessing as to the kind of 'human conduct' to which hard rock can lead. The *Daily Mirror* reports that 'A night out at a rock concert ended in tragedy for schoolboy Chris Tyrer. He died after joining in a "head banging" session. It is the dance in which youngsters shake their heads from side to side in time to the music. Chris was seen "head banging" as 1,000 fans watched the rock group Saxon at Wolverhampton Civic Hall. The next morning his parents found him paralysed down one side. He died in hospital eight days later.'[32] Even more horrendous is the story of Mark Silman. The teenager from Tilehurst, Reading, a former Elvis Presley fanatic, killed a fifteen-year-old girl by stabbing her eighty-five times with a ten-inch butcher's knife. The *Reading Chronicle* reported that he had modelled himself on a rock singer with the group The Meteors, who sing about blood and violence and drink blood on stage.[33]

These cases may be extreme, but they are certainly not unique — and we can assume that there are countless other young people who are being physically damaged because of exposure to the kind of sound rock singer Ted Nugent had in mind when he said, 'Rock is the perfect primal method of releasing our violent instincts.'[34] Yet so many Christians seem strangely oblivious to the danger. The Christian musician Keith Green, tragically killed in a plane crash, once wrote, 'I have to say that I have never once seen a case where music was the direct cause of sin or wickedness in a person's life.'[35] The evidence says otherwise, and leads to the obvious question: has any Christian, whose body is 'a temple of the Holy Spirit' (1 Corinthians 6:19) the right, for the selfish satisfaction of his own musical tastes, to expose himself for even one moment to the kind of music that can potentially lead to such consequences?

It's all in the mind

Not only can rock music be physically damaging, another area of danger is that it opens the door to *psychological manipulation*. Dr William Shafer is quite blunt about it: 'Rock music is a tool for altering consciousness.'[36] So is Robert Palmer of the *New York Times*, who claimed that using music to induce altered states of consciousness had become one of the most significant musical trends of the nineteen-eighties and that rock musicians were beginning to explore the possibilities of rhythmic and modal repetition, which seeks through absolute control of limited musical means to induce certain psychological states. In their book *Super Learning*, Sheila Ostrander and Lynn Schroeder write, 'The idea that music can affect your body and your mind certainly isn't new . . . For centuries, from Asia to the Middle East to South America people have used music to carry them into unusual states of consciousness. The key has always been to find just the right kind of music for just the right kind of effect.'[37]

The Communist regimes have made intensive studies into ways of conditioning people. One Bulgarian doctor, after fifteen years' research on the use of music in conditioning says, 'Certain drumbeats act as a kind of pacemaker, regulating brain-wave rhythms and breathing, which leads to biochemical changes that produce altered states of consciousness. If you listen to a different drummer, you do see a different world.'[38] In a remarkable book called *The Science of Yoga*, I. K. Taimni comes to the same conclusion: 'There is a fundamental relationship between vibration and consciousness, because each level of consciousness has a specific vibration associated with it.'[39] In his book *Subliminal Seduction*, Wilson Bryan Key tells of advertising companies spending fortunes researching how music can be used to influence people. Some discovered that a seventy-two-beats-a-minute rhythm increases suggestibility and that a television commercial with such a beat produced the headache symptoms that the product being advertised was supposed to cure.[40]

But the evidence for psychological manipulation does not come from outside sources alone. Rock musicians have been saying the same thing for a long time, though in simpler, cruder ways. Timothy Leary was certainly on to it: his song 'Turn on, tune in, drop out' became an anthem for millions, and Leary's comment on it was 'Don't listen to the words, it's the music that has its own message . . . I've been stoned on the music many times . . . the music is what will get you going.'[41] Graham Nash said, 'Pop music is *the* mass medium for conditioning the way people think.'[42] Pop singer Donovan agreed: 'Rock music is the music for affecting consciousness.' Drummer Spencer Dryden was quite clear how this power should be used: 'Get them when they're young. Bend the minds.'[43] Mick Jagger said much the same thing: 'We're moving after the minds and so are most of the new groups.'[44] In *Melody Maker* he said, 'Communication is the answer to the whole of the world's problems and music is the key to it all because music opens the door to everybody's mind.'[45]

High or deep?

Of course it is not only rock music that can be used in

psychological manipulation. The same can be true of classical music. Hitler used some of Wagner's music to crank up the crowds — and even parts of Handel's *Messiah* when he wanted to create a pseudo-religious atmosphere. Even the best of music can be used from the worst of motives.

One secret of music's great power is that it appeals so directly to the subconscious. As a result, people soak up the meaning of music without being aware that they are doing so. Add to that the volume level, constant repetition and incessant beat which are so much a part of rock music, and the scene is set for the conditioning process. As Cedric Cullingford wrote in *The Guardian*, 'Far from being a palpable alternative culture with its own clear ideas, pop music is something absorbed at a subconscious level.'[46] Many young Christians have told us that they feel perfectly safe in listening to records containing perverted lyrics because 'We don't listen to the words, we just happen to like the music.' But they have missed the vital point that the music *itself* is affecting them at an even deeper level *without their knowing it*. As Wilson Bryan Key has written, 'The unconscious system appears to be able to unscramble even certain kinds of distorted information without individuals becoming consciously aware of the perception.'[47] In another study he adds this even more disturbing comment: 'Anything consciously perceived can be evaluated, criticized, discussed, argued and possibly rejected, whereas unconsciously perceived information meets no resistance or qualification by the intellect.'[48]

Surely the dangers of all this are obvious — and not least in communicating the gospel! Evangelists have sometimes been told during a lively gospel concert, 'Don't worry, we'll bring them down before you speak.' But why do the listeners need to be 'brought down' before hearing the gospel? What were they 'up' on? An emotional 'high'? Then why were they taken up there? Presumably as a preliminary to the preaching! The whole thing becomes a tragic nonsense. Why is it important to get a crowd 'high'? That kind of conditioning amounts to trying to do the work of the Holy Spirit for him. There is certainly a right kind of preparation for the hearing of God's Word, but excessive volume, driving beat, repetitious phrases and the like are not the biblical way to go about it. Musical conditioning is not the same as the Holy Spirit challenging the mind to think, the spirit to be still and the heart to be humbled in the presence of God.

In closing this chapter, let us ask a very important question. In loading our evangelistic programmes with manipulative music, are we not greatly increasing the risk of producing 'conversions' that are psychological rather than spiritual? The set-up could not be more perfect. Impressionable young people can undoubtedly be so conditioned by the music that they are much more likely to accept whatever the preacher says. Add a good communicator and the chances are that he will produce an impressive number of 'decisions'. However, the danger is that these 'decisions' are the result of musical conditioning rather than spiritual conviction. We will take a closer look at this in the next chapter. 'But evangelists can be manipulators too,' somebody says, 'even those who do not use a great deal of music.' Yes they can — and when they are, the eventual results are just as disappointing. It would not be difficult to prove that the best 'manipulators' among evangelists are among those who produce the most impressive immediate statistics — but the numbers that count are those that continue.

Everybody enjoys music of one kind or another. Add its power to stir the emotions of its listeners, recognize the fact that rock music in particular is such a tremendous attraction to young people, and the idea of using it in the work of evangelism seems obvious and natural. But evangelism is not about the natural; it is about the spiritual. We are serving a God who says, 'My thoughts are not your thoughts, neither are your ways my ways' (Isaiah 55:8) and in evangelism, as in every other area of life, the all-important thing is not to go along with the majority, not even the Christian majority, but to 'find out what pleases *the Lord*' (Ephesians 5:10).

6.
Pop goes the gospel

If 'Christian music' does not actually exist, nobody seems to have told today's church! Within the last hundred years a thriving tradition of music has taken root in its evangelistic programme. The most popular movement in Britain was fired to a large extent by the work of Ira D. Sankey, civil servant turned gospel musician, who accompanied the great American evangelist D. L. Moody to this country on his evangelistic campaigns in 1873. Five years later William Booth founded the Salvation Army and wrote, 'Every note, every strain, and every harmony is divine and belongs to us . . . bring out your cornets and harps and organs and flutes and violins and pianos and drums, and everything else that can make a melody. Offer them to God, and use them to make all the hearts about you merry before the Lord.'[1] The reverberations were loud and long, but the real explosion was to come eighty years later.

Rock hits the road

As we saw earlier, rock 'n' roll arrived on the scene in the early nineteen-fifties. Very soon, it swept around the Western world, and before long Christians were beginning to see it as a potential vehicle for the gospel. Today, the emphasis on pop music in British evangelism, especially among young people, is almost overpowering, with advertisements for musical events, 'happenings', celebrations, festivals, concerts and 'gigs' cramming the pages of the popular Christian youth press.

The religious road show has become a major feature, with an apparently endless succession of musical tours around the country. At one given moment, we found current notices for over 500 one-night stands and other musical events. Not that they have been unanimously welcomed — many ministers pressurized into encouraging their churches' support have come away disillusioned. Bill Spencer, editor of *Evangelism Today*, wrote, 'As tour after tour drags our young people away from reality the time has surely come for people to make their objections known. Is it too much to hope that the young will somewhere be able to hear a word from God without the use of banks of loudspeakers and flashing lights?'[2]

Then there are the 'static' events: the Greenbelt rock festival attracts over 20,000 people; Spring Harvest is heavily laced with music and several other more 'traditional' gatherings are leaning in the same direction. Alongside the tours and the larger set pieces a whole industry has sprung up, kept solvent by thousands of young Christians who cheerfully keep the cash flowing in for records, tapes, tickets, posters, stickers, T-shirts and other associated paraphernalia.

Question time

But in the absence of biblical examples for this kind of evangelism it is surely important to ask some questions. What motivates the musicians? What prompts the promoters? Are we to imagine that they are all devil-inspired 'moles', infiltrating the Christian church in order to destroy it from the inside? Of course not —

though it goes without saying that in an industry of this size there are bound to be rogues of one kind or another. Not all of those involved in hyping the teenage market do so from motives that are pure as the driven snow. Some of the performers would not even claim to be Christians. Tom Morton, a full-time musician with British Youth for Christ, writes quite openly about this: 'What has happened over the last fifteen years in Britain has been the formation of a Christian music "scene", featuring record companies, management agencies, tour organizers, full-time performers, concert promoters and assorted hangers-on. Instead of this subculture being rooted in Christian standards in fact as well as in name, it appears that some of the Christian music scene has become, in effect, sub-Christian. Some Christian musicians seem excessively concerned with fame, with their image; some record companies seem profit-orientated at the expense of their artists' ministries, and since their "package" is wrapped up in pseudo-evangelical language and justification, few people have realized what was happening.'[3] Elsewhere, he makes this frank admission: 'The rock music industry is perhaps one of the most corrupt in existence, and the unthinking transfer of its techniques to the Christian sphere has resulted in some of the uneasy mixtures of gospel and garbage which have in the past gone under the name of "gospel concerts".'[4]

Motives under the microscope

Those are serious statements — and they are made by someone who knows the Christian pop music scene from the inside — but let us be as positive as we can and assume that the vast majority of those in the gospel pop scene are sincere Christians seeking to serve God

through gospel music. What reasons do they give for
believing that they are right in doing so?

1. 'It draws the crowds'

There is certainly no question about that. The huge
crowds that attend pop gospel concerts easily out-
number those attending gatherings centred on preaching.
But should that surprise us? In the first place, pop
music has become an indispensable part of today's
youth culture. Many teenagers are immersed in their
music. It is an identity mark — and the gospel pop event
gives the young Christian an apparently irresistible
opportunity to express his Christianity in this way
without resisting the pressure of his cultural group.

Secondly, Christian pop makes no spiritual, moral
or ethical demands. It is essentially presented as entertainment, something to be enjoyed — and pop gospel
musician John Allen knows where that leads: 'It seems
undeniable that most of the audience is there simply to
enjoy the music, not to think hard about anything;
and there is a real danger of the emergence of the
"Greenbelt Christian", the semi-converted, shallowly
committed teenager whose Christianity means little
more than that he enjoys festival-going.'[5] That is a
very significant admission even if, as Allen claims, the
organizers are aware of the problem.

Thirdly, we are living in a time of spiritual depression,
when the church has a much greater appetite for the
trivial and amusing than for the biblical and searching.
If we are honest, A. W. Tozer's words have an undeniable ring of truth about them: 'It is scarcely possible
in most places to get anyone to attend a meeting where
the only attraction is God.'[6] But that must never be an
excuse for conceding to man's lack of spirituality. As
Paul Bassett says, 'One of the subtlest ways of flattering
man is to communicate the gospel in a way he wants
rather than the way he needs.'[7]

Having said all of that, the claim about popularity is irrelevant, because our real concern should be with truth and principle, not voting figures.

2. 'It communicates to young people in a language they can understand'

Agreed! There is no doubt that pop music *does* communicate, and that what may seem to be disjointed lunacy to 'golden oldies' is a definite language to the 'in' crowd. Like all other music, pop is bound up with its culture. In this case it is the culture of the young and there are times when its language is virtually unintelligible to others.

Taking all this for granted, the big question is whether pop music communicates the *gospel* in this way. We maintain that it does not, for the crucial reason that the medium has a distorting influence on the message. David Hesselgrave makes this point very powerfully in a statement which does not have pop music particularly in mind: 'Missionaries must divest themselves for ever of the naive notion that the reception of the gospel message is the same irrespective of how it is conveyed to the world — whether by book, magazine, radio, television, film, sound recording, etc. Perhaps no fiction has had wider currency than if you put a gospel message into any of these media at one end, it will come out at the other end as the same message . . . *The media must always affect the message.*'[8]

To return to pop music: does *this* communicate the gospel effectively and without distortion? After all, it is vitally important that the message of the gospel is not only biblically given but biblically received. Now the Bible's primary appeal is to the *mind*: God appeals to men: 'Come now, let us *reason* together' (Isaiah 1:18); Christ's summary of the First Commandment

includes the need to 'love the Lord your God . . . with
all your *mind*' (Mark 12:30); Paul makes it clear that
the way to prevent conformity to the world is 'by
the renewing of your mind' (Romans 12:2). Yet, as
Graham Cray admits, 'In all pop music lyrics are second-
ary. Pop is music of feeling, spoken primarily to the
body and only secondarily to the intellect.'[9]

That is a very significant statement — made by an
expert in the field — and it is backed up by singing
superstar Larry Norman: 'In order to decide whether
Christian music has any great weaknesses or strengths
you have to decide what its purpose is. If it's for non-
Christians — to convince them that Christ is an important alternative to seek in their life — then most
Christian music is a failure because *it doesn't con-
vincingly communicate that particular message.*'[10]

There is another and much more important point
to be made here and that is that the Bible makes it
clear that the unconverted man *cannot* understand the
gospel: 'The man without the Spirit does not accept
the things that come from the Spirit of God, for they
are foolishness to him and he cannot understand them,
because they are spiritually discerned' (1 Corinthians
2:14). Not that this gives us an excuse for sitting back
and doing nothing. We must do all we can to communicate clearly, forcefully and persuasively — but at
the end of the day only the Holy Spirit can carry the
truth into the mind, the heart, the conscience and the
will. So to say that the unconverted teenager 'under-
stands gospel rock' is a dangerous half-truth. He may
understand rock (whatever may be meant by 'understanding' it) but he certainly doesn't understand the
gospel.

3. *'Music is essentially neutral and is coloured only by
the words'*

This is undoubtedly one of the strongest arguments put forward in favour of gospel rock – and we must therefore give it very careful attention. These two statements summarize what is being said. In Larry Norman's words, 'The sonic structure of music is basically neutral. It's available to anyone to express any kind of message they choose.'[11] To quote John Fischer, 'Basically, music is neutral. Art forms are neutral.'[12] In a private discussion, one of today's pop gospel superstars suggested to us that the first music heard on earth might have been a raindrop falling on a tautly-drawn leaf. He then suggested that as that was neutral and created by God all music was both neutral and God-given. But to jump straight from a raindrop to a rock concert and to lump them together with everything in between is frankly naive. It is obvious that a single *note* (Dictionary definition: 'a tone of a definite pitch')[13] does not of itself have any influence, good or bad. It has neither message nor meaning. In that sense, we agree that it is 'neutral'. But the debate is not about single, isolated notes, but about *music* (Dictionary definition: 'the art and science of combining tones in varying melody, harmony, etc. so as to form complete and expressive compositions').[14] The words 'expressive compositions' are important – they tell us that when single notes or tones are deliberately brought together in a musical work they are no longer neutral. When music is composed, it is not composed into a neutral nothing, but into a positive something – a form that is definite and meaningful, with colour and character.

We can illustrate the same principle by comparing music to the printed word. The text of Psalm 23 in the New International Version has 437 letters of the alphabet. Before they were assembled by the printer, these letters were neutral. They were complete and perfect, but they meant nothing, they had no message.

But in Psalm 23 they have been grouped together to
form an expressive composition. Now they are saying
something, and the order in which they have been
composed precisely determines what they are saying.

Take those same 437 characters, arrange them differ-
ently, and instead of spelling out a message of assurance,
comfort and faith for the Christian believer they could
spell out a message of hate, greed or violence. Com-
pose them in some other way and they would form a
shopping list. The individual letters would be the same,
but they would have lost their neutrality in the composition. The American popular scientist Benjamin
Franklin once said that with twenty-six lead soldiers
he could conquer the world. The lead soldiers were the
letters of the alphabet and Franklin's point was that
when assembled together in the right numbers and in
the right order they had power to change men's lives.
Once assembled, the soldiers would no longer be
neutral — nor are musical notes and tones when
assembled into an expressive composition.

The point is so important that it is worth listing a
number of statements to back up our contention that
music is not neutral. Firstly, let us listen to some comments on music in general, spanning centuries of time.
Plato (428–348 B.C.), the outstanding Greek philosopher, wrote, 'Musical training is a more potent instrument than any other, because rhythm and harmony
find their way into the inward places of the soul.'[15]
Aristotle (384–322 B.C.), Plato's most famous student,
wrote, 'Music has the power to form a character.'
Boethius (c. 480–c. 524) the Greek philosopher and
statesman, wrote, 'Music is a part of us, and either
ennobles or degrades our behaviour.'[16]   John Calvin
(1509–1564) wrote, 'We know by experience that
music has a secret and almost incredible power to
move hearts.'[17]   Coming to the present time, one

authority after another could be quoted along the same lines. To repeat words we quoted earlier from Sheila Ostrander and Lynn Schroeder: 'The idea that music can affect your body and mind certainly isn't new . . . The key has always been to find just the right kind of music for just the right kind of effect.'[18] Cyril Scott adds this: 'Music affects the minds and emotions of mankind. It affects them either consciously or subconsciously, or both. It affects them through the medium of suggestion and reiteration. It affects them either directly, indirectly, or both.'[19] Dr George Stevenson, Medical Director of the National Association for Mental Health, Inc., says, 'The widespread occurrence of music among widely distributed people and various cultures is evidence that in music we have a great psychological force.'[20] Dr Howard Hanson, Director of the Eastman School of Music at the University of Rochester, says, 'Music can be soothing or invigorating, ennobling or vulgarizing, philosophical or orgiastic. It has powers for evil as well as for good.'[21]

Over and above all of these statements, we have the overwhelming testimony of human history, with all its evidence that music has moved man in a hundred different ways. It has calmed his fears, summoned up his courage, soothed his sorrows, stimulated his memory, stirred him to violence, prepared him for death.

There is also a striking illustration of the power of music in the Old Testament, when we are told in 1 Samuel 16 that King Saul called for David to play his harp to him during his recurring bouts of melancholia. We are then told that 'Whenever the spirit from God came upon Saul, David would take his harp and play. Then relief would come to Saul, he would feel better, and the evil spirit would leave him' (1 Samuel 16:23).

To suggest in the light of all that evidence that

music in general has no influence is to swim against a
very strong tide indeed!

But what about rock music, which is our primary
concern? Does it share this kind of influence? Bob
Larson has no doubts about that: 'Teenagers are
immersed in their music, and their philosophies are
being formed by the lyrics, the call to action in the
beat, and the personal opinions of rock idols . . . On
occasion I have been accused of overstating the effect
of rock music. Many sociologists, however, now believe
that there is no other factor doing more to influence
teenage folkways, values and morals . . . we of the
mass communications generation live under the unprecedented influence of a formidable formulator of
human thought.'[22] Professor Frank Garlock agrees:
'No other single influence has done as much to shape
the standards and moral conduct of today's teenagers
as rock 'n' roll.'[23] Writing in *The Guardian*, Cedric
Cullingford speaks of school teachers' reactions to pop
music, and says, 'Of all the mass media, pop is the one
that is most often cited by them as influencing children.'[24] Later on in the same article he writes, 'In a
study of nearly 500 children it was clear that their
tastes changed very rapidly according to the state of
play of *Top of the Pops*.'[25]

We have stressed this particular point because the
issue is tremendously important in considering the
whole subject of rock music and the gospel. We leave
it with these clinching words by Dr Max Schoen, in
his book *The Psychology of Music:* 'Music is the most
powerful stimulus known among the perceptive senses.
The medical, psychiatric and other evidences for the
non-neutrality of music is so overwhelming that it
frankly amazes me that anyone should seriously say
otherwise.'[26]

One further point: if music is neutral, if it can say

whatever the hearer wants it to say, then why are certain kinds chosen as background music played on airplanes, in supermarkets, or in places likely to be stressful? If music is neutral, why would we consider the theme music from Alfred Hitchcock's film *Psycho* unsuitable to be played in dentists' waiting rooms? The obvious reason is that the music is chosen *to do something*; and the reason it can do something is that it is not neutral.

4. 'There is a distinctive difference between Christian rock and secular rock'

This argument is strongly advanced by some of those with interests in the religious pop scene, but other thoughtful observers disagree. Rock singer Chuck Girard, for instance, makes this honest admission: 'If you took the lyrics away and changed them to a secular message, I don't think you would be able to tell the music apart from pop, rock-orientated music.'[27] Steve Turner went even further when in 1973 he told readers of *Buzz*, 'The difference between a Slade concert and many Jesus rallies is negligible.'[28] Eight years later Professor Verna Wright reported that when gospel and secular rock records were played in a controlled test held in a Belgian youth club, the hearers 'couldn't tell the difference'.[29] This exactly confirms the contention of Dr William J. Shafer, who says,'Rock is *communication without words*, regardless of what ideology is inserted into the music;'[30] and of Professor Frank Garlock, who says, 'The words only let you know what the music *already says* . . . *The music is its own message* and it can completely change the message of the words.'[31] What all of this is saying is that rock music is rock music, not just a plastic medium that can be bent in any direction. Even John Fischer, who believes that music is neutral, admits that 'Some art forms have been created to express certain philosophies *and are*

*so wedded to those philosophies that they convey that
kind of outlook.*'[32] Even more significantly he adds,
'We can't assume that we simply plug in a Christian
message and everything will be okay.'[33]

Surely it is not difficult to relate this to today's pop
gospel scene? Perhaps these words by Richard Taylor
sum up the fatal flaw in the argument that religious
rock is somehow different: 'We cannot change the
basic effect of certain kinds of rhythm and beat simply
by attaching to them a few religious or semi-religious
words. The beat will still get through to the blood of
the participants and the listeners. Words are timid
things. Decibels and beat are bold things, which can
so easily bury the words under an avalanche of sound.'[34]

5. 'It produces excellent results'

It certainly seems to. The popular Christian press reports
dozens and sometimes hundreds of 'decisions' registered
at a single pop gospel event and the immediate, visible
results from road-show religion seem to relegate the
effect of straightforward preaching to that of a badly
beaten also-ran. But is that the whole story – or even the
real story? Let us dig behind the headlines.

In the first place, the pragmatic argument is simply
not valid. We gladly accept the sovereignty of God in
salvation, and do not deny that in his gracious wisdom
he has saved young people and others in gospel rock
concerts – but the fact that God uses any means is not
of itself any indication that it is biblically valid. As
Franky Schaeffer points out, in condemning poor quality
in Christian art forms, 'The excuse that "sometimes
people are saved" is no excuse at all. People have been
saved in concentration camps because God can bring
good from evil, but this does not justify the evil.'[35]

God is God and can use anybody and anything for
any purpose he chooses – but his use of them does not

make them right. God used the Egyptian ruler
Ramases II as an instrument in releasing the entire
nation of Israel from slavery in Egypt — and told him
in the process that 'I have raised you up for this very
purpose, that I might show you my power and that my
name might be proclaimed in all the earth' (Exodus
9:16). Yet Ramases II was a godless tyrant and
certainly not an example for us to follow. Moses got
excellent results when he struck the rock at Meribah-
Kadesh and produced enough water for the entire
Israelite community and all their livestock — but God
condemned and punished him for what he did.

We need to learn and relearn the lesson. The pressure to produce has eaten deeply into the fabric of the
church and, as Eric Wright puts it, 'The evangelists'
methods and the results they perceive have become
the theology of evangelism . . . and woe betide the one
who tilts at this "sacred cow".'[36] But we *must* tilt at
it, and constantly remind ourselves that every aspect
of evangelism must be ruled by biblical principles.
In Dr J. I. Packer's words, 'When evangelism is not
fed, fertilized and controlled by theology it becomes
a stylized performance seeking its effect right through
manipulative skills rather than the power of vision
and the force of truth.'[37]

Let us take a look at the results said to be produced
by pop gospel evangelism. Do they bear close examination? To try to assess this, we explored them in three
areas.

In the first place, we conducted a census among 1,829
young people in England, Wales, Scotland and Northern
Ireland between the ages of 14 and 25 (the group most
thoroughly exposed to the pop gospel idiom), asking
them to indicate the circumstances in which they
were converted or the major influence in their conversion. The young people concerned came from

churches of seven major denominations in both urban and rural areas. Some of the churches were specifically involved in the pop gospel scene, others were not. The poll indicated that of the 1,829 young people concerned, only 39, or 2.1%, were converted at a gospel concert. (Even this tiny figure almost certainly gives an exaggerated picture; the poll did not ask whether the musical presentation was the specific means of conversion.)

Secondly, we tried to obtain what we might call a 'middle-term' assessment of the results claimed by the religious road shows that have toured Britain during the past two years or so. This proved somewhat difficult, as in many cases figures are not available. However, we do know of an instance in which over 200 'decisions' had dwindled to four by the time a follow-up meeting was arranged a few weeks later and of others where the leakage had been just as serious. In the same general area of road-show religion we know of a school at which 100 'decisions' were recorded in the course of a band's 'ministry' there — yet a short time later the only lasting effect seemed to be that one of the students concerned showed 'a mild interest' in Christian things.

Thirdly, we wrote to eleven major missionary societies (chosen in alphabetical order from the UK Protestant Missions Handbook) asking for an indication of how many of their candidates had been converted or called into full-time Christian service in a pop gospel context. Here are the relevant extracts from their replies.

'From our experience we have not had any missionary candidates approach us for service who have come to know the Lord through such means.'

'We have found few, if any, people who have come to faith through this sort of musical presentation.'

'I cannot call to mind anybody who has been converted through this type of youth evangelism and has subsequently gone on to missionary service.'

'Over the years I have interviewed quite a number of men for the mission and I cannot recall any one of them indicating that the Christian pop scene has been at all influential in their conversion or Christian life.'

'I certainly do not know of anyone who has come into the mission through the musical pop scene.'

'None of our candidates appears to have been converted in the sort of atmosphere you describe.'

'As far as we can tell, we have not had any candidate who has been converted through this kind of evangelism.'

'I do not think that we have sent anyone to the field whose conversion during the last five years could have been attributed to evangelical road shows.'

'We have not had any applicants for missionary service over the past five years who were converted through entertainment evangelism.'

'The simple answer to your question is "No".'

'As far as we can tell none were converted at such meetings.'

Another missionary society which heard about our enquiries wrote, 'We have nobody amongst our candidates (and at the moment we have about 35) who were influenced by pop concerts.'

In addition, we received the following unsolicited
note from a minister who knew of our enquiries and
who had until recently been closely connected with a
major missionary society not included in our sample:
'You may be interested to know that I spent ten years
majoring in candidate interviewing and selection. I recall
not one incident of a pop concert featuring in a conversion or call. It may have, but I recall none and in
recent years I was more alert to this possibility.'

These facts and figures are not only disturbing but
alarming. The pop gospel scene in Britain today is a
high-powered, multi-coloured, glossily packed, heavily
promoted industry — but it seems that when the music
stops, the applause dies down, the lights go out, the
cash is counted and the show moves on, what is left is
only a microscopic fraction of what seemed to be.
When there is that kind of difference between the headline and the bottom line, something, somewhere, is
seriously wrong. It is time to strip the bandwagon down
and start again.

7.
Square one

Discussion on a controversial subject can begin almost anywhere — with a news item, perhaps, or a well-known person's opinion, or an obvious change in trends. But for the Christian there is one fundamental principle that should govern all his thinking and ultimately determine his decisions.

Anything from God?

About 589 B.C. a man called Zedekiah was the puppet King of Judah, then held in captivity in Babylon. He was a nasty piece of work, and we are specifically told that neither he nor any of those he influenced 'paid any attention to the words the Lord had spoken through Jeremiah the prophet' (Jeremiah 37:2). He even allowed Jeremiah to be imprisoned on a trumped-up charge of trying to desert to the Babylonians. But when the going got really tough he sent for him and asked him one crucial question: 'Is there any word from the Lord?' No doubt the place was buzzing with all kinds of rumours and speculation. There must have been dozens of ideas as to the cause of Judah's problems, and just as many as to what the solution might be. But when the chips were down Zedekiah knew in his heart that there was only one thing that mattered: *what does God say?*

It's in the book

For today's Christian, Zedekiah's question can be put
like this: 'What does the Scripture say?' (Romans 4:3).
The Christian is not left at the mercy of his feelings on
matters of either belief or behaviour. God has not only
spoken but has caused his words to be written down
for us to read, study, understand and obey. In the
Bible's own words, 'All Scripture is God-breathed and
is useful for teaching, rebuking, correcting and training
in righteousness, so that the man of God may be
thoroughly equipped for every good work' (2 Timothy
3:16). This means that the Christian should come to
the Bible not as a *last* resort (ransacking it to find statements which he hopes will back up his own opinions)
but as a *first* resort (so that his views will be grounded,
governed and guided by a word that 'stands firm in
the heavens' (Psalm 119:89)).

Many of the great Christian leaders over the centuries have expressed this submission to Scripture in
memorable ways. Augustine, who died in A.D. 430,
yet remains one of the most influential Christians in
history, once said, 'We must surrender ourselves to the
authority of the Holy Scripture, for it can neither mis-
lead nor be misled.' Martin Luther wrote, 'Before the
Word everyone must give way.' John Calvin said, 'The
Bible is the sceptre by which the heavenly King rules
his church.' And John Wesley claimed, 'I am a Bible
bigot. I follow it in all things, both great and small.'
Yet we must not think of that kind of philosophy as
being the special achievement of spiritual giants. This
is *normal* Christianity. Opinions are interesting, trends
are significant, arguments are fascinating, but the
Christian must be governed by God — and that means
being governed by Scripture. As the seventeenth-century
preacher William Gurnall said, 'The Christian is bred by

the Word and he must be fed by it'! The Christian who
is determined to begin at square one must put away
his newspapers and magazines and sit down with his
Bible.

Five hundred plus

Trying to find a specific reference to particular subjects
in the Bible is sometimes like trying to find the proverb-
ial needle in a haystack. (Not that that makes those
references unimportant; God does not have to repeat
himself for his words to have authority.) What is more,
some important subjects are mentioned surprisingly
seldom: for instance, there are no more than four
references to the Lord's Supper in the whole of the
Bible. When we come to the subject of music, the
situation is quite different. The Bible contains no
fewer than 550 references to music, musicians and
musical instruments, and our problem is not where to
find them but how to assemble and understand them.

In the beginning – singing stars

Although the Bible is scientifically accurate, it is not a
scientific textbook, and its accounts of the creation bear
this out. They are extremely brief and sometimes
almost lyrical. For instance, speaking of the creation of
the world, God asks Job, 'On what were its footings
set, or who laid its cornerstone – while the morning
stars sang together and all the angels shouted for joy?'
(Job 38:7.) No doubt the phrase about stars singing is
metaphorical, but surely it is also *meaningful*? If God
can speak of the pure response of his created works to
the majestic glory of his creation in terms of song,

surely singing must be something which God welcomes
and in which he delights?

That's an order!

We can confirm God's approval of music by noticing
the many times when the inspired writers of Scripture
command his creation to praise him in song. Here are
some examples: 'Let the heavens rejoice, let the earth
be glad; let the sea resound, and all that is in it; let the
fields be jubilant, and everything in them. Then all the
trees of the forest will sing for joy; they will sing before
the Lord' (Psalm 96:11, 12). 'Let the rivers clap their
hands, let the mountains sing together for joy; let them
sing before the Lord' (Psalm 98:8). 'Praise the Lord, all
his works everywhere in his dominion' (Psalm 103:22).
Again, however metaphorical all this may be, it is
clearly something God ordains and desires, and if these
were the only biblical references to music and singing
we had they would be sufficient for us to know that
music has a God-given place in his universe.

All people that on earth do dwell

If stars and trees, mountains and rivers are told to praise
God, we should surely expect to find the same response
demanded from man, the crown of God's creation —
and we do, on page after page. Here are just some of the
dozens of instances we could quote: 'Sing to the Lord,
you saints of his; praise his holy name' (Psalm 30:4).
'Sing joyfully to the Lord, you righteous; it is fitting for
the upright to praise him. Praise the Lord with the harp;
make music to him on the ten-stringed lyre. Sing to him
a new song; play skilfully, and shout for joy' (Psalm

33:1–2). 'Shout with joy to God, all the earth! Sing to the glory of his name; offer him glory and praise!' (Psalm 66:1–2). 'Sing to the Lord! Give praise to the Lord!' (Jeremiah 20:13).

These references are nearly all in what we might call a 'general' context, but many others are more specific, with people being told to sing praise to God for his goodness to them in particular circumstances, for special blessings received, for deliverance from their enemies, and so on. Even more important than the context is the *focal point* of all this worship, praise and thanksgiving, which is *God himself*. In fact, God and the praising music of his people are so wrapped up together that Moses and the Israelites could sing, 'The Lord is my strength *and my song*' (Exodus 15:2). As they celebrated their miraculous deliverance from the hands of the Egyptians, their song of praise had God not only as its object and inspiration, but as its theme. In the fullest possible sense, their song was sung to the glory of God.

God's gift

Another factor we must note, in this general look at the place of music in Scripture, is that music is not only *for* God but *from* God. In praising God for delivering him from a difficult situation, David says, 'He put a new song in my mouth, a hymn of praise to our God' (Psalm 40:3). Even that one reference is important! It tells us that it is not enough to think of music merely in terms of human culture but of divine creation. Music is certainly an art, but it is primarily a *gift*. As John Calvin once put it, 'All arts proceed from God and ought to be held as divine inventions.'[1] Elsewhere, Calvin goes on to say, 'Among other things adapted for men's

recreation and for giving them pleasure, music is either
the foremost, or one of the principal; and we must
esteem it a gift from God designed for that purpose.'[2]
A number of years earlier Martin Luther said the same
thing more colourfully: 'Music is to be praised as second
only to the Word of God because by her are all the
emotions swayed . . . When natural music is sharpened
and polished by art, then one begins to see with amaze-
ment the great and perfect wisdom of God in this
wonderful work of music . . . He who does not find
this an inexpressible miracle of the Lord is truly a clod
and is not worthy to be considered a man!'[3] We agree
with them both. No Christian can legitimately be
opposed to music *per se*. He may prefer one style or
type to another, but to reject music out of hand is to
run contrary to God's intention for him, and to be
less than the whole person God wants him to be.

The farmer, the musician and the toolmaker

There are those who believe that the first reference to
any subject in the Bible is of particular importance,
and this would certainly seem to be so in the case of
music. It comes just a few generations removed from
Adam and Eve, when the Bible tells us about the three
sons born to Lamech and his two wives, Adah and
Zillah. This is how they are introduced: 'Adah gave
birth to Jabal; he was the father of those who live in
tents and raise livestock. His brother's name was Jubal;
he was the father of all who play the harp and flute.
Zillah also had a son, Tubal-Cain, who forged all kinds
of tools out of bronze and iron' (Genesis 4:20—22).
Now that sounds like nothing more than part of somebody's family tree, but there is much more to it than
that. What is so important about it is that these three

brothers were obviously the 'founding fathers' of three important groups of people. The first was a farmer and the third a toolmaker — and agriculture and industry are obviously vitally important for man's well-being. But the middle brother was a *musician*, with the obvious inference that man is more than just a food-eating worker. He has other dimensions beside the physical and material — and the needs of one of those other dimensions are properly met by music. In the words of the American classical pianist Sam Rotman, 'Here, within the compass of but a few verses, God reveals that the provision of man's material needs is not enough; in addition, man must have an outlet for his aesthetic sensitivities. Even from the beginning music was more than a mere pastime which could be viewed as something pleasant but essentially unnecessary. Simply stated, God has created in man a certain aesthetic need which can be best satisfied in music, and in his love and wisdom he has provided for this need.'[4]

Music is not merely something that is potentially pleasant; it is something essential to the total needs of total man — and God has lovingly provided man with the ability to exercise his gifts in order to create it. The picture is simple and beautiful. The very existence of music should cause us to praise the God who gave it to us.

Feelings and faith

We ought at this point to ask ourselves one very basic question about music: *what is it for*? Put very simply, the answer is that music is one of the ways by which man can give audible expression to his common emotions — joy, sorrow, love, sympathy, heroism, compassion, and so on — and as we turn the pages of

the Bible, beginning with the Old Testament, we find it
used in all of these areas. In Erik Routley's words,
'Music was in very wide use in the culture of Israel at all
its stages . . . we can distinguish epics and dirges in
secular contexts (insofar as any context for Israel was
secular), and songs of praise, thanksgiving, instruction,
personal experience, and liturgical significance in the
religious context.'[5]

Yet most Bible references to music occur in direct
connection with the worship and service of God; with
man's religious faith rather than with his 'general'
feelings. The first of these references is in Exodus 15,
where we have the great 'freedom song' of Moses and the
Israelites. By the time we reach 1 Chronicles religious
music has become highly sophisticated and organized,
with King David appointing no fewer than 4,000 singers
'to praise the Lord with the musical instruments I have
provided for that purpose' (1 Chronicles 23:5) and 288
master musicians 'trained and skilled in music for the
Lord' (1 Chronicles 25:7).

Nor must we forget that the Psalms formed a 'hymn-
book' for Old Testament believers, with some of the
instructions (which are part of the text of Scripture)
being quite specific in giving details of the musical
instruments to be used. Psalm 4 has the note, 'with
stringed instruments', and Psalm 5 'for flutes' — presumably to ensure that the music matched the words.
What fascinating 'forewords'! God was not to be
worshipped in a slapdash way. Great care was taken
to meet certain criteria.

The point is important, because many of those
involved in gospel music today would point back to
the highly organized music of the Old Testament and
claim that it gives them all the licence they need for
'doing their own thing' — but closer examination tells
a different story. It has been pointed out that of the

eight musical instruments in use by the Israelites, only four (harp, lyre, cymbal and horn) were specifically authorized for use in the temple. Timbrels were taboo, as were flutes, pipes and dulcimers — though these are mentioned in the Psalms and could properly be used elsewhere. What is more, the musicians had to come from certain families, they played only on certain limited and special occasions, and only at specific times during the service. There was no question of a free for all, with anyone who could play an instrument being invited to join the band and turn the service into a music festival. Instead, music was rigidly controlled in the temple worship, presumably to ensure it was never the predominant factor. The broader lesson is that neither in music, nor in any other area of life, has God given us licence to 'do our own thing'.

What happened to the hyssop?

But the pop gospel musician who tries to lean on chapter and verse in the Old Testament has further problems, because if he continues reading his Bible he soon discovers that all of that musical organization was a purely temporary arrangement. It was part of the Old Testament ritualistic and sacrificial system that was abolished by the death of Christ. All the paraphernalia of temple worship, though ordained by God, was part of a system of types, figures and shadows that was done away with when Christ instituted the new covenant. Those who justify their musical activities purely on the grounds that musical instruments were used in Old Testament worship could find the same justification for putting tassels on their clothing, asking God to purge them with hyssop, walking about Zion and waving bits of dead rams! Would it not be more biblical to agree that all of these types, systems, rituals and sacrifices (ordained by God to accommodate the particular spiritual darkness of Old Testament times) have now been abolished, and replaced by the simple beauty of Christ's statement that true worshippers are those who worship 'in spirit and in truth' (John 4:24)?

The New Testament

What is extraordinary about the 500 musical references in the Bible is that they are virtually all in the Old Testament. The other remarkable division we must note is that of all the New Testament references, only ten or so refer to Christians here on earth (the others being to the heavenly hosts mentioned in Revelation) and of these two are quotations from the Old Testament. Of the remainder two merely tell us that Jesus and his disciples sang a hymn before they left the Upper Room to go to Gethsemane (Matthew 26:30; Mark 14:26); one that while in prison at Philippi, Paul and Silas were 'praying and singing hymns to God' at midnight (Acts 16:25); and another that Paul was determined to sing God's praises in a language that could be understood by the hearers (1 Corinthians 14:15). There was 'music and dancing' in the parable of the prodigal son (Luke 15:25), while James gives the simple instruction: 'Is anyone happy? Let him sing songs of praise' (James 5:13).

That leaves just two places in the whole of the New Testament where there is direct instruction given on the subject – and they are parallel passages, saying virtually the same thing. Writing to the Ephesians, Paul says, 'Speak to one another with psalms, hymns and spiritual songs. Sing and make music in your heart to the Lord, always giving thanks to God the Father

for everything, in the name of our Lord Jesus Christ'
(Ephesians 5:19). Writing to the Colossians he says,
'Let the word of Christ dwell in you richly as you teach
and admonish one another with all wisdom, and as you
sing psalms, hymns and spiritual songs with gratitude
in your hearts to God' (Colossians 3:16).

Notice the identical lists Paul mentions: psalms,
hymns and spiritual songs. What were these? 'Psalms'
would be mainly, but perhaps not exclusively, the Old
Testament Psalms as we know them; 'hymns' would be
current compositions in praise of God the Father and
the Lord Jesus Christ (we may have snatches of some
of these here and there in the New Testament); while
'spiritual songs' seemed to have covered a rather wider
range of lyrical compositions, but could have included
the other two groups.

And that's it! The New Testament has nothing else
to say on the subject. Yet even these brief phrases have
lessons for us. In the first place, variety is encouraged
in Christian worship. As Derek Kidner puts it, 'Our
garden of praise, if we may put it so, is not to be all
vegetables, or even all one kind of flower.'[6] Secondly,
however, variety does not mean licence to do anything
we please. 'Psalms' and 'hymns' had direct reference
to God, but the songs, too, had to be 'spiritual' – an
important qualification. Music about God should reflect
his glory, beauty, holiness and order, and should direct
men to him and to his ways. Thirdly, as the nineteenth-
century preacher and commentator Albert Barnes
wrote, 'The prevailing character of music in the worship
of God should be *vocal*. If instruments are engaged,
they should be so subordinate that the service may be
characterized as *singing*.'[7]

Each of these principles is important. The Bible says
we are to do 'all for the glory of God' (1 Corinthians
10:31) – and we do not do this by merely tacking

God's name on to something, any more than adding
'in the name of Jesus' to a prayer makes it audible in
heaven or effective on earth. To use music for God's
glory is to use music that draws attention to him, that
mirrors his majesty, and that meets all the biblical
criteria we have before us. Quite apart from anything
else, this means that we should take any composition
of words or music to Philippians 4:8 and ask these
questions: 'Is it true? Is it noble? Is it right? Is it pure?
Is it lovely? Is it admirable? Is it excellent? Is it praiseworthy?' If it fails to meet these standards, we have
no right to use it in God's service.

Eloquent silence?

Before we leave our look at music in Scripture, there
is one final point to make — one which may at the
end of the day prove to be the most decisive of all.
In all of the Old Testament references, there is not
one instance of music being used to help communicate
Judaism to the heathen.There is no record, for instance, of
the Israelites organizing a Jewish religious folk festival to
try to convert the Hittites, Hivites, Jebusites or Amale-
kites! Even more significantly, there is no reference
in the New Testament to the early church using music
to reach non-Christians with the gospel (though music
was obviously available to the church). All the references are to the church at worship; there are none to
the use of music in evangelism.

Surely that is very striking? Here is the church,
bursting with new life, longing to tell the world about
the risen Christ. Here are its Spirit-filled leaders, willing
to give everything, even their own lives, to reach men
and women with the gospel. Here is the apostle Paul
saying, 'I have become all things to all men so that by

all possible means I might save some' (1 Corinthians 9:22). Yet we never once read that they used the powerful medium of music to get their message across. Did they miss the boat – or did they know something we have either forgotten or ignored?

Of course, there are those who will say, 'But that is an argument from silence.' Yet if we are absolutely honest we have to ask ourselves this question: is the silence saying something – something crucially important?

8.
Yours sincerely, Concerned

When the American evangelist D. L. Moody visited Scotland for his great evangelistic campaigns in 1873 his partner was Ira D. Sankey, whose organ playing and singing attracted great crowds. But when the team went to hold a Sunday afternoon service in Glenorchie Church, Edinburgh, church leaders took one look at the organ and said, 'We're no havin' such a kist fu' o' whistles in our kirk,' and promptly dumped it out on to the street! When prejudice is in control reasoning is usually rationed!

Throughout this book we have tried to give *reasons* for everything we have said. We are not 'knocking' music, not even pop music as a whole, *but we are concerned*. We are concerned for the glory of God, which should always be the ultimate aim of every Christian. We are concerned for the good of the church, all of whose members are our brothers and sisters in Christ. We are concerned for the integrity of the gospel; we don't want to see it dragged in the mud. We are concerned for the spiritual welfare of young Christians, who are sometimes so cynically manipulated by an older generation. In this chapter we want to 'earth' some of these concerns in certain areas of pop music evangelism.

What's the difference?

Firstly, we are concerned that the pop gospel idiom can

so easily encourage *worldliness*. To find out what we mean, read these two paragraphs.

'This is music to hit yourself on the head to. Who cares if the lyrics are a bit simple, even banal in places? The album runs from solid rock through to electric blues and ends up at heavy metal. There are times when the female vocalist sounds like Janis Joplin and at others her voice is like wailing banshees in the night.'

'They're the sort of people that my mother told me not to play with. I bet they spit on buses! You won't like this album if you're any kind of weed . . . It's that nasty, noisy, loud heavy metal stuff. Not unlike Quo. Very roots rock 'n' roll. Sounds in places like lunatic music. Exciting, throbbing, subversive rock 'n' roll — just like it should be. Can you describe head-banging as intellectual? . . . Good stuff — buy it!'

Where do you think those quotations are from? *New Musical Express? Sounds,* perhaps? Wrong and wrong, in that order! They come from the Christian youth magazine *Buzz.* The first is a review of the album 'Barnabus' by Hear the Light[1]. The second is a review of a record by a band called 100% Proof.[2] Yet in the same issue Scripture Union has a full-page advertisement including them in 'twelve of the best' records currently available.[3] Even more astonishingly, and again in the same issue of *Buzz,* this 'nasty, noisy, loud, heavy metal' band is included in an advertisement for Spring Harvest, billed as 'six days of relaxation and teaching to help you to build God's Kingdom in your locality'![4]

Here is an advertisement for another group: 'Ear smacking, flame quenching, hot-rocking, light showing, different sounding, health damaging, gospel telling, crowd pulling — *Rock Salt.* '[5] Substitute 'story' for 'gospel' and that could be an advertisement for the most vulgar or destructive band playing today. Only

one word separates it from that — and our concern is
that the difference *is* no more than a word and that
the spirit is the same as that of the world. An avalanche
of adjectives may be good promotion, but is it
scriptural? We get the same picture in the Greenbelt
literature. Here is a report on the group Tense: 'Their
huge visual assault and presence engendered an electric
atmosphere. The visual pinpoint is the girl singer, clad
in black, bending low like a stalking animal, or standing still, head thrown back. "The Bunker Song" was a
perfect showcase for her evident talent, the full bodied
voice sweeping low over the music, almost snarling,
bringing an icy edge to the song.'[6]

From the same issue, this is what was said about a
song by Mystery Guests: ' "Take a look at yourself" was
good, clean, solid pop and featured Carrie Watt in a
skimpy red dress and elbow length black gloves. She
bopped around for all she was worth and threatened
to go straight through the stage at any moment.'[7]

Without making any judgement on the sincerity or
integrity of anyone involved, the question we want to
ask is this: what kind of *spirit* does all of this suggest?
Doesn't it seem to be one which is merely aping the
world — using its language, its values, its images? The
emphasis on the performance, on the singer's dress,
gloves, actions, 'bopping' ability — is this spiritual and
helpful or sensual and unhelpful? To avoid being mis-
understood, let us make it clear that we are not making
a distinction between spiritual and *physical*. Man is
body, mind and spirit and all can be engaged in spiritual
activities. The Bible makes this perfectly plain: 'Offer
your bodies as living sacrifices, holy and pleasing to
God — which is your *spiritual* worship' (Romans 12:1).
The question we are asking is whether a religious cloning
of show-business presentation makes it spiritual or leaves
it as it was — worldly. There is a difference between

being animated and anointed. As Bob Larson rightly puts it, 'Clothing and choreography will never make the gospel appealing. Great men of the faith have been martyrs, not swingers.'[8]

Let us take this a little further. The Bible makes it clear that we are not to dress or behave in ways that might create moral problems for other people. When 'secular' singers do so, we are right to condemn what they do. Then can we excuse the Christian pop star when he unbuttons his shirt, wears skin-tight leather trousers and wiggles his buttocks at the audience? What is the difference? Do the 'Jesus words' in the songs sanctify his actions?

This highlights one of the greatest problems in Christian pop, the fact that it blurs the gap between Christian and non-Christian value systems by trying to incorporate them both. Let us illustrate it further. In September 1982 *Buzz* carried a major feature on the singer Charlene (though in *Buzz* she became 'the dark-haired cool-as-a-glacier-mint' Charlene!). While recording a 'Christian' album news came that a song she had recorded in her pre-Christian days was suddenly climbing the charts. *Buzz* reporter Gill Twyman enthused, 'Charlene had hit the number one spot! The studio, a converted Primitive Methodist chapel, shook with almost as much excitement as Wesley's visits probably generated two centuries ago.'[9] Yet the lyrics of her chart-topper went like this: 'I've been undressed by kings and I've seen some things that a woman ain't s'posed to see, and I've spent my life exploring the subtle whoring that cost too much to be free'!

The comparison could hardly be more distasteful. The success of a piece of musical pornography is equated with the spiritual revival which followed the preaching of a man of God whose aim, in his own

words, was 'to spread scriptural *holiness* over the land'.
Can we seriously imagine John Wesley joining in what
Buzz called 'the euphoria' that followed the news about
that mucky song? This blurring of the basics is just one
of the things that makes the pop gospel idiom so potentially damaging.

Who's number one?

Our second concern is that rock music evangelism
encourages *exhibitionism*. Writing a number of years
ago in the old British Youth for Christ magazine *Vista*,
Ben Ecclestone, in an article entitled 'Rape of the Ear',
said, 'All musical performance carries with it a built-in
temptation to put on an act,' and there is no doubt that
he is right. Provided one isn't petrified with fear, there
is something powerfully attractive about going on stage
in front of a crowd. We know this to be true as evangelists and believe the danger to be even greater for
musicians, whose appeal is so much more directly to the
emotions.

Exhibitionism is basically one area of worldliness
and rock musician Keith Green was in no doubt that
many Christian artists had failed to get it right. In *Can
God use Rock Music?* he wrote, 'Frankly, I have been
just as much offended by most of what I've heard and
seen as any sweet ole Christian grandma who accident-
ally stumbles into a blaring-loud gospel concert . . .
It isn't the beat that offends me, nor the volume —
it's the spirit. It's the "*look at me!*" attitude I have
seen in concert after concert, and the "Can't you see
we are as good as the world?" syndrome I have heard
on record after record.'[10]

This tendency to act as stars instead of servants is
clearly reflected in the kind of advertising and review

material published in the popular Christian youth press. For example, the following comments all appeared in one issue of *Buzz*: 'A fantastic feast of rock and praise'; 'the finest Christian music'; 'leading Christian artists'; 'highly talented newcomers'; 'unbelievable'; 'British Christianity's biggest, most energetic and certainly loudest event'; 'top stars'; 'extraordinary entertainment'.

How does that kind of language tie in with the apostle John's statement that 'The cravings of sinful man, the lust of his eyes and *the boasting of what he has and does* comes not from the Father but from the world' (1 John 2:16)? Is it not also faintly ridiculous? To make the point, we have taken three advertisements from *Buzz* and substituted our own names for those of the musical performers. This is the result: 'John Blanchard is one of Britain's most popular Christian preachers. His personality, distinctive oratory and powerful sermons are now world famous. His most recent sermon, "How I found humility" looks destined to reach the very top for style and popularity'; 'What stimulates the grey cells, gives your feet a treat and does your ears a favour? All of those who answer "Heineken" leave the room immediately. The answer is Peter Anderson, with his multi-media sermon entitled "Whose side are you on?"'; 'Derek Cleave has the distinction of being a catalyst for some of the best preaching performances in the world. His achievements and experiences as part of the famous Christian Ministries team is clearly evident in the way he preaches.' Would that kind of nonsense be acceptable in advertising our meetings? If not, why not? And if not, why should it be acceptable in any part of God's service? The apostle Paul's approach was exactly the opposite: 'For we do not preach ourselves, but Jesus Christ as Lord, and ourselves as your servants for Jesus' sake' (2 Corinthians 4:5).

The star syndrome is accentuated by *Buzz*'s annual
Rock Poll, which invites its readers to vote for the 'Best
UK Album', 'Best American Album', 'Best Male Vocalist', 'Best Female Vocalist', 'Best Up and Coming Band'
and so on. This may seem perfectly harmless, but is it?
Is it helpful to the readers (listeners) to concentrate
their thoughts in this way on the performance of the
artists? Is it helpful to the artists themselves to be the
centres of this kind of attention?

Any honest Christian knows that genuine humility
is hard to come by. Fighting pride is a constant and
costly struggle. To a greater or lesser extent we all
have an appetite for appreciation, a liking to be lauded.
Voting for musicians on the basis of how professionally
they perform in playing and singing about the one who
deliberately 'made himself nothing, taking the form of a
servant' (Philippians 2:7) is not only unhelpful to all
concerned but a total contradiction of a central truth
of the Christian faith.

Dr Alan Redpath, one of the 'senior statesmen'
among British evangelical preachers, puts his finger on
the spot in his book *Blessings out of Buffetings*: 'The
principle of the world is "self-glorification" and the
principle of the Christian is "self-crucifixion". The
principle of the world is "exalt yourself" and the
principle of the Christian is "crucify yourself". The
principle of men is greatness, bigness, pomp and show;
the principle of the cross is death . . . There is never a
breaking through of communication of [Christ's] life
in your heart and through you to others in heavenly
conviction and authority which will challenge or bless
them unless at that point there has been a personal
Calvary.'[11] The application of this to the pop gospel
performer is surely not difficult? One of the inherent
problems about the idiom is that the attention is focused
firstly on the singer and then on the song — whereas the

object of evangelism is to get the attention focused on
the Saviour. We can come at this from another angle.
When trying to convey a verbal message to someone,
it is *unnatural* to back up the words by swaying,
squirming, dancing, slinking or gyrating various parts
of one's anatomy. When these things are done on stage
they are an act, part of a show – and showmanship on
the part of a gospel communicator (preacher or singer)
is an abomination. His sole duty is to point people to
Christ; to draw attention to himself not only fails to
help in getting the gospel across, it positively hinders
any attempt to do so. It also places the performer in
a dangerous position in the light of God's very clear
statement: 'I will not yield my glory to another' (Isaiah
48:11). There is no questioning the fact that the pop
gospel idiom encourages exhibitionism. In Michael
Green's words, 'What we need is not just a message
of crucifixion, but the crucifixion of the messenger.'[12]

On with the show?

The third concern we have is that gospel pop is presented as *entertainment*. This is undoubtedly one of
the 'crunch' issues on the whole subject and we will
therefore need to look at it thoughtfully, carefully
and *honestly*. Let us begin by getting our definitions
clear.

Firstly, what do we mean by *'entertainment'*? The
verb 'to entertain' has at least twelve different mean-
ings,[13] but we can soon whittle the list down. Five are
now obsolete and can immediately be dropped; again,
'to entertain' can mean to provide food or shelter, to
treat hospitably, to take something into consideration,
to hold something in the mind, or to meet or experience something – none of which really applies here.

That leaves us with three: 'to hold the attention or thoughts of', 'to hold the attention of pleasurably' and 'to amuse'. We suggest that it would be perfectly fair all round to say that neither the first nor the third of these fits the gospel pop bill. On the one hand, music's primary appeal to the emotions makes the first definition somewhat exaggerated; on the other hand 'to amuse' is commonly associated with making fun, and although some gospel pop performers do take unbiblical liberties in that area, it would be unfair to tar them all with the same brush. That leaves us with 'to hold the attention of pleasurably'. To use the dictionary's noun, 'entertainment' in this sense is 'a performance or show intended to give pleasure'[14] — and we suggest that that is a perfectly fair description of pop gospel evangelism.

Secondly, what is the *gospel*? As every Christian knows, the word simply means 'good news', but it is important to remember that it is not good news about the possibility of a better life-style or how to solve life's problems; nor even about the possibility of shaking off a guilt complex and 'feeling great'. Essentially, the gospel is good news about a *Person,* the Lord Jesus Christ. In what were possibly the first New Testament words ever written, Mark calls it 'the gospel about Jesus Christ, the Son of God' (Mark 1:1). The apostle Paul constantly refers to it as 'the gospel of Christ' (Romans 15:19; 1 Corinthians 9:12; 2 Corinthians 2:12; 9:13; 10:14; Galatians 1:7; Philippians 1:27; 1 Thessalonians 3:2). The insistence is important! There is no gospel apart from Christ, there is no gospel without Christ and there is no gospel outside of Christ. Elsewhere, Paul calls it 'the gospel of the glory of Christ, who is the image of God' (2 Corinthians 4:4). An 'image' (or likeness) is something that can be seen, and Paul's words emphasize the point that the gospel is a combination of who Christ is and what Christ did. These are the essential elements of the gospel — *and there is nothing entertaining to be found in any of them.*

There is nothing entertaining about the eternal deity of Christ, bathed in the glory he had with his heavenly Father 'before the world began' (John 17:5). There was nothing entertaining about his coming into the world, 'taking the very nature of a servant, being made in human likeness' (Philippians 2:7). There was nothing entertaining about his miracles; they were performed 'for God's glory so that God's Son may be glorified' (John 11:4). There was nothing entertaining about his lifelong struggle against temptation; he '*suffered* when he was tempted' (Hebrews 2:18). There was nothing entertaining about his prayer life; we are told that 'he offered up prayers and petitions with loud cries and tears' (Hebrews 5:7). There was nothing entertaining about his experience in the Garden of Gethsemane, when 'his sweat was like drops of blood falling to the ground' (Luke 22:44). There was nothing entertaining about his agonizing death on the cross when the burden of our sin forced him to cry out, 'My God, my God, why have you forsaken me?' (Matthew 27:46). There was nothing entertaining about his resurrection, by which he was 'declared with power to be the Son of God' (Romans 1:4). There was nothing entertaining about his ascension into heaven, when he was 'taken up in glory' (1 Timothy 3:16). There will be nothing entertaining when he returns to earth, when 'every eye will see him, even those who pierced him' (Revelation 1:7). There will be nothing entertaining when all of humanity stands before him on the day of judgement and when as 'judge of the living and the dead' (Acts 10:42) he will pronounce men's eternal destinies.

If not one single element in the gospel message is entertaining, how can the gospel possibly be presented

as entertainment? The life of Jesus was not a religious
road show; he did not come to give a performance,
but to give his *life*! At the end of the day, this is the
fatal flaw in entertainment evangelism – it is a contradiction in terms. The object of entertainment is to give
pleasure (and there is nothing essentially wrong with
pleasure), but the object of evangelism is to warn man
of his appalling spiritual condition and to point him to
the one who 'came into the world to save sinners'
(1 Timothy 1:15). As Paul Bassett rightly says, 'The
danger is just as great today as it was in Paul's day of
producing a crossless Christianity whose flattering
appeal creates fans, but not followers.'[15]

The whole thing becomes even more absurd when
we realize that although the gospel is good news, it
does not appear so to the sinner. The Bible speaks of
'the offence of the cross' (Galatians 5:11); it describes
Christ as 'a stone that causes men to stumble and a
rock that makes them fall' (1 Peter 2:8); it says that
'The message of the cross is foolishness to those who
are perishing' (1 Corinthians 1:18) and that the message
of a crucified Saviour is 'a stumbling block to Jews
and foolishness to Gentiles' (1 Corinthians 1:23). To
the unconverted, the glorious message of the gospel is
sheer nonsense; to tell him that his only hope of the
forgiveness of sins and eternal life lies in the hands of
a young Jew who was murdered and rose from the
dead 2,000 years ago insults his intelligence, offends
his sense of decency and hurts his pride. Then how
can we do these things and *entertain* him at the same
time?

All of this underlines the seriousness of the work
of evangelism. The apostle Paul could tell the Ephesians, 'I served the Lord with great humility and with
tears' (Acts 20:19) and 'I never stopped warning each
of you night and day with tears' (Acts 20:31). Can the

evangelistic entertainer honestly claim to have that kind of burden? In the work of evangelism, the church is a lifeboat, not a showboat!

(Perhaps we need to put a paragraph in parenthesis here. In pointing out the fundamental folly of entertainment evangelism we are not suggesting that the Christian message is one of gloom and doom, best presented by people with personalities and styles to match. After all, the Bible says that 'The kingdom of God is not a matter of eating and drinking, but of righteousness, peace and joy in the Holy Spirit' (Romans 14:17). But the order of those key words — 'righteousness', 'peace' and 'joy'— is not accidental. The Christian life is certainly meant to be one of *joy*, but a Christian's real joy depends on the extent of his *peace* (of heart, mind and conscience), while his peace depends on his *righteousness* (his right relationship with God). To offer joy before peace, and peace before righteousness, is to put both carts before the horses. There is never true joy without peace and no real peace without righteousness. So the *first* aim in evangelism is not to bring joy (let alone superficial happy feelings) but to bring home to people the need to get right with God. As Dr Martyn Lloyd-Jones said, 'The business of preaching is not to entertain but to lead people to salvation, to teach them how to find God'.)[16]

Artists or ambassadors?

Larry Norman, one of the best-known performers ever to appear on the pop gospel scene, has virtually admitted the impossibility of combining entertainment and evangelism. Asked, 'What is the main aim of your ministry?' he replied, 'I don't think music is a ministry. Music is just a bunch of notes.'[17] Later in the same interview, when asked what he was trying to achieve through his music, he said, 'I *never* achieve evangelism through my music. If I'm going to say anything evangelistic, I say it with words and not music. Music is art, not propaganda.'[18] Larry Norman's honesty is helpful. Pop music aims at pleasing people, evangelism aims at saving them. Pleasing people is a perfectly legitimate aim, of course – in the right context. Holiday Inn, the international chain of motels, call themselves 'The People Pleasin' People' and no doubt they have countless satisfied customers to say that that's fine. But pleasing people must never be a factor in evangelism. One of the principles that governed New Testament evangelism was this: 'We must obey God rather than men' (Acts 5:29). Paul could say, 'We are not trying to please men but God, who tests our hearts' (1 Thessalonians 2:4) and a moment later, 'We were not looking for praise from men' (1 Thessalonians 2:6).

This poses a constant and fundamental problem for the gospel pop singer. He *is* trying to please men, but the idiom he is using is one that imposes what we might call 'popularity pressure' – *his* popularity. The publicity, the spotlights, the presentation, the applause – all the attention is on him rather than on his message. When John the Baptist was preaching, his stage was the desert, he wore his ordinary clothing, his message was clear and uncompromising, he made no attempt to please men and his attitude was one of utter humility. We might almost say that it was the most natural thing in the world for him to point to Jesus and say, 'Look, the Lamb of God' (John 1:29). It is almost impossible for the gospel pop singer to have that same spirit, because of the pressures the idiom imposes on him. However sincere his motives, however genuine his personal devotion to the Lord, whatever his songs are saying, what so often comes across is not 'Look, the Lamb of God', but 'Look at *me* saying, "Look, the Lamb of God".' His real dilemma is put in a nutshell by David Porter when he says, 'The problem is that art was never meant for preaching with at all.'[19]

The shallow end is dangerous

Our fourth concern is that entertainment evangelism can so easily reduce the gospel message to *triviality*. This comes across in a great deal of the advertising for gospel concerts and the like. To speak about 'star-spangled entertainment' and 'extravaganzas' (we quote from *Buzz*) may bring in the crowds, but the language is a far cry from Gethsemane and Golgotha.

The pop idiom also tends to trivialize the message. The late Keith Green had a song called 'Dear John (Letter to the Devil)' in which he sang,

Well I believe in Jesus
And what he said he's gonna do.
He'll put an apple in your mouth
And cook you in a sulphur stew.

No doubt the fans raved about that, but the Bible teaches that it is both wrong and dangerous to use that kind of language about Satan. The apostle Jude tells us that when the archangel Michael was disputing with the devil about the body of Moses he 'did not dare to bring a slanderous accusation against him, but said, "The Lord rebuke you!"' (Jude 9). If it is wrong and dangerous to use that kind of language about Satan, it is even more so when singing about any of the Persons in the Godhead. 'You can't keep a good man down' may be a very 'pop' way of singing about the resurrection of Christ, but it is theologically trivial and biblically criminal. Countless other gospel pop songs are equally trivial in

content, not only as far as the doctrines of God are
concerned, but also those concerning man's response to
the gospel. Graham Kendrick admitted this when speaking at Spring Harvest in 1979: 'One of my criticisms of
those of us who use music in evangelism is the nature
and content of the "gospel" which is preached. All too
often, a superficial kind of believism is offered, along
with promises of large helpings of love, joy and peace.'
He then went on to suggest that the triviality was not
only in the songs but in the singers: 'One can only
assume that many of us preach this because our own
commitment or understanding of discipleship is superficial.' Even more revealingly, he went on to speak of
those with a 'happy go lucky, anything will do, attitude
towards the business of bringing new spiritual babes to
birth'. Fellow musician Garth Hewitt agreed: 'An
analysis of the lyrics of *most* gospel songs indicates a
very superficial view of salvation and of Christianity.'
(The italics are ours – but the information is his.)
When two of the leading personalities in today's pop
gospel scene go on record as saying that most of the
material being used is very superficial, surely we are
right to be concerned at the sheer triviality that the
pop idiom encourages?

   We can give a vivid and recent illustration of this.
For some time in 1983 *Buzz* ran a promotion campaign
to encourage new readership. Those taking out a year's
subscription to the magazine were offered a double
album called 'The Four Side Saga' at a bargain price.
The collection of thirty-two tracks was given the full
adjectival treatment: 'the finest contemporary Christian
music gathered from around the world'; 'major house-
hold names'; 'remarkably talented newcomers';
'a genuine exploration of the best in today's Christian
music' and 'a voyage of discovery into the best Christian
music on release'.

So much for the fanfare — what about the facts? As
a fair sampling, we listened to the first eight tracks.
Paradise have as their 'gospel' the refrain, 'Trust in
him and feel alright'; Frontline repeat, 'My, my, my,
what a wonderful world' thirty-two times in two-and-a-
half minutes, accompanied by raucous (and dubbed)
applause; The Predators' message is 'I'm a plastic sur-
geon . . . and he carries a bottle of cyanide . . . He's a
person of change . . . he's going to rearrange you';
Larry Norman's punchline is 'Jesus is the rock that
rolled my blues away'; Resurrection Band sing, 'I can't
get you out of my mind' thirty-one times, with no
indication as to who 'you' is; The Barratt Band's 'Playing in the City' has no recognizable Christian reference;
Crowd Control sing of people as houses made of flesh
and bone; and Steve Flashman tells us, 'I live in slow
motion with all my devotion . . . I've lots of time to
improve.'

The question we want to ask is simple, serious and
sincere: is there any valid connection whatever between
that collection of songs and biblical Christianity? As far
as we can honestely tell, there is scarcely one suggestion
of anything remotely scriptural in them from beginning
to end. Yet they are being heavily promoted as 'the *best*
in today's Christian music'. *Buzz* headlines the offer
with the words: 'This is a rip-off'. Quite unintentionally,
that hits the nail right on the head!

The truth or the tune?

Our fifth concern is that reliance on the pop gospel
idiom betrays *a lack of faith in the gospel*. If the idiom
has so many weaknesses and dangers, why go on using
it? The argument of many is that young people will
not listen to the gospel presented in any other way.

Youth leaders and others have said as much to us: 'We'll need to get a band, or the young people won't listen. Music is the only way we can reach them.'

Is that true? Is there any other *serious* subject that we would insist needed to be communicated by music before it could be understood and accepted by young people? Imagine an eighteen-year-old employed by a company that insists on an annual medical check-up for all its staff. He seems very fit and has no sense of need, but goes reluctantly to hospital when his time comes. After a careful examination, the doctor discovers that the young man is suffering from a serious disease that will prove fatal unless he receives immediate and radical treatment. Can you imagine the doctor asking his assistant to set the man's disease to music, rustle up a few nurses, plug in some musical instruments and then get them to sing the diagnosis to the patient — *because that would be the best way to get through to a teenager*? The idea is absurd — yet time and again we are told that you must have music before young people will listen. We could extend the illustration: if the pop music medium is so effective at communicating to young people, why not use it in schools, colleges and universities? Why not give biology some beat, jazz up geography, get into heavy metal history and liven up languages by doing them in a disco? The reason is obvious and the same in each case: the medium does not fit the message. As an expert in the pop gospel field has admitted to us, 'Music does not lend itself to presenting the facts of the gospel in the ordered, sequential way which is to be required if there is to be a thoughtful response.'

This being the case, let us ask some straightforward questions. Is it true to say that it is the *unsaved* who insist on the music? Or is it nearer the truth to say that it is young *Christians* who enjoy it so much that they insist on it? Is it true that unconverted friends of Christians adamantly refuse to attend any evangelistic presentation except a musical one? Or is it truer to say that they are almost never asked? Isn't it true that young Christians invite friends to gospel concerts as a first resort rather than as a last resort? When told that music was the only way to get through to young people today, an evangelist friend of ours replied, *'Have you never heard of the Holy Spirit?'*!

The pop idiom has virtually become a life-support system for youth evangelism in Britain today, and we believe that one of the reasons for this is that Christians have lost that naked faith in the power of the gospel that was the hallmark of the early church. Dr Alan Redpath made the following comment to us on this particular point: 'The growing tendency to the sensual appeal of rock music is one of the tragedies of our time. People tell us that the church has lost touch with the world. That is nonsense. The fact is we have lost touch with *God*, and when we do that we resort to every possible alternative to put on a programme, one of which is the very heavy slant towards rock music. It is the outcome of wrong priorities in the church. We will not see revival as long as we offer Christian entertainment to people. The Holy Spirit is not in that business.' If that diagnosis is right, then a great deal is wrong!

Messiah with blow-waves

Our sixth concern is that the pop idiom *tends to water down the gospel.* In his book *The Divine Conquest,* A. W. Tozer writes, 'If I see aright, the cross of popular evangelicalism is not the cross of the New Testament. It is, rather, a new bright ornament upon the bosom of a

self-assured and carnal Christianity. The old cross slew
men; the new cross entertains them. The old cross
condemned; the new cross amuses. The old cross
destroyed confidence in the flesh; the new cross
encourages it.'[20] In *Of God and Men* he adds this:
'Much that passes for New Testament Christianity is
little more than objective truth sweetened with song
and made palatable by religious entertainment.'[21]
Those are serious charges, but we believe them to be
true. Of course, Tozer is referring to church life in
general, but his comments particularly apply to the
popular music scene. There are essential elements of
biblical truth that cannot be fitted into the narrow
and shallow confines of a pop gospel idiom. Can a
pop song explain what is meant by God, sin, judgement, the death of Christ, faith or justification? And
if not, how can it convey the gospel? Geoff. Thomas
goes so far as to say, 'It is impossible to communicate
the gospel of Romans in music, dance or drama.'[22]
The pop gospel approach has another problem in this
area: doctrines such as the sovereignty of God, the
depravity of man, the substitutionary death of Christ,
the need for genuine repentance and the call to holiness of life cut and hurt and offend the natural man.
He *hates* these things. How then can they possibly be
conveyed to him in an entertainment idiom, which is
designed to be pleasurable to his senses? You cannot
touch a man's heart by tickling his ears. Dr J. Sidlow
Baxter makes this comment in his book *Re-thinking
our Priorities*: 'Pop style, lilty, swingy airs or strum-
mings simply do not fit the rich, deep, urgent, serious
truths of the Bible and the gospel.'[23] In other words,
the music does not fit the message. The music may be
popular, but as Erik Routley says, 'If any music is
composed or performed with an eye simply to attract-
ing the unconverted, it is likely to fall into the same

error we find in the parson who, in order to make users of bad language feel at home, uses bad language himself.'[24]

One of the results of trying to convey the whole biblical picture by pop music is that you end up only conveying part of it — which means that the listeners receive a fragmented message instead of a full one. All too often the end result is that people *do* enjoy hearing the 'gospel', because it has been tailored to suit their wants rather than to meet their needs. They are quite happy to 'make a decision for Christ', because the Christ they have heard about is not the Christ of Scripture — he is the kind spoken about by Stewart Henderson (adopting a persona) in his poem 'Splintered Messiah':

I don't want a splintered Messiah
In a sweat-stained, greasy grey robe;
I want a new one.
I couldn't take this one to parties;
People would say, 'Who's your friend?'
I'd give an embarrassed giggle and change the
    subject.
If I took him home, I'd have to bandage his hands.
The neighbours would think, 'He's a football
    hooligan.'

I don't want his cross in the hall;
It doesn't go with the wallpaper.
I don't want him standing there
Like a sad ballet dancer with holes in his tights.
I want a different Messiah, streamlined and
    inoffensive,
I want one from a catalogue,
Who's as quiet as a monastery.

I want a package-tour Messiah, not one who takes
me to Golgotha.
I want a King of kings with blow-waves in his hair.
I don't want the true Christ;
I want a false one.[25]

All too often, that is the one the listener gets. The
real Christ is still 'despised and rejected by men' (Isaiah
53:3). That is what makes him such poor 'box office'.

Focus on the family

Our seventh concern is that the pop idiom *widens the
generation gap*. Rock 'n' roll was the first music in the
history of the world specifically aimed at the teenage
market. Its beat appealed to their awakening senses. It
spoke of rebellion, revolution, freedom, independence —
and the more adults objected to it, the more the young
took it to their hearts. It became an international
anthem for young people and a major factor in estab-
lishing the 'youth culture' we have today.

An advertisement placed by Rolling Stone in the *New
York Times* said, 'Rock and roll is more than just music.
It is the energy centre of a new culture and youth revolution.'[26] Bob Dawbarn wrote in *Melody Maker,* 'Rock
'n' roll, if not actually inventing the teenager, split the
pop followers into the under twenties and the rest.'[27]
The Beatles' George Harrison made it clear that aliena-
ting adults was no accident: 'Music is the main interest
of the young people. It doesn't really matter about the
older people now because they're finished anyway.'[28]
Prominent music critic George Lees was even more
specific: 'Rock music has widened the inevitable and
normal gap between generations, turned it from something healthy — and absolutely necessary to forward

movement — into something negative, destructive,
nihilistic.'[29] Jazz artist Ira Gitler agreed: 'Above all
other considerations, rock is definitely the music of
today's youth and its importance is more social than
musical . . . It sets them apart from the values and
attitudes of the adult, establishment world in a more
emphatically schismatic manner than ever before.'[30]

It is not difficult to see that philosophy reflected in
the life of the church, with young people becoming
increasingly segregated from the rest of the congre-
gation. We believe that this tendency to create a 'youth
church' is unnatural and unhealthy. The Christian
church is a family and the members of a family ought
to demonstrate their common solidarity, rather than
their differences. In a healthy home all the members
of the family eat together, not at different times (unless
working hours or other factors require this). Nor is
there any such thing as 'youth food'. Nobody markets
'teenage baked beans'. Should there not be a parallel in
the church? Of course, we are not suggesting that there
should be a law demanding that every Christian should
have the same musical tastes — that would be absurd.
What we are saying is that rock music has always placed
an unnatural emphasis on 'youth culture' as a separate
entity in society and that such an emphasis is damaging
to the life of the church. This is not empty theorizing;
we have seen its effect in countless churches during the
past twenty years. Yet there is no such thing as a 'youth
church', nor is there a 'youth gospel'. There is '*one* body
and *one* Spirit . . . *one* Lord, *one* faith . . .' (Ephesians
4:4–5). Christians are 'all *one* in Christ Jesus' (Galatians
3:28). Nothing should be encouraged which tends to
blur that beautiful picture.

Yours sincerely, Concerned

These are some of our major concerns about the pop
gospel idiom; there are others which we cannot develop
more fully here.

As with other music, gospel rock *tends to blur the
need for doctrinal clarity*. For example, an outspoken
Roman Catholic can share a gospel concert at the Royal
Albert Hall with singers and musicians who are equally
outspoken evangelicals. Would the Reformation martyrs
have gone along with that?

It *detracts from the unique place God has given to
preaching*. Nearly twenty years ago, Ben Ecclestone was
concerned enough about the trend to write this in
VISTA: 'One of the unfortunate tendencies of present-
day evangelism is that it has given to gospel beat music
an unprecedented place of favour over the preaching of
the Word of God. We have been mistakenly led to
believe that today, above everything else, we must have
music; any music, but beat music in particular. How
very far from the truth this is.' The situation is certainly
no better today. Preaching has got pushed further and
further out of its biblical place, and when that happens
to anything we have problems. As David Marshall puts
it, 'When preaching in church life retreats before music;
to that extent church life itself is retreating from New
Testament ground, and moving into the perilous terri-
tory of mere human opinion and tradition.'[31] Later in
the same article he suggests that where biblical
principles are followed,'music modestly retreats to a
subordinate place before the majesty of the Word'.[32]

We also believe that the pop idiom *tends to project
a substitute gospel*. A great deal of it concentrates on
man's felt needs — his loneliness, emptiness, sadness,
lack of fulfilment. The songs then invite the hearers to
'come to Jesus' for joy, peace, thrills, happiness, a

'high'. New Testament preaching never does this; it addresses itself to man's *real* spiritual condition — lost, dead, a rebel, an enemy of God. Man's need is not to get 'turned on' but to get turned around.

Finally, we believe that the preoccupation of young people with the pop gospel idiom *discourages personal evangelism*. The heavy emphasis on organized events and stage performances tends to turn young Christians into listeners rather than communicators. For countless numbers of them, evangelism has become a spectator sport. Larry Norman certainly recognizes this: 'This whole Christian thing has burgeoned into some dilettante art form . . . The singers are doing one album a year and a lot of concerts and they're so popular. The audience is buying the Album of the Month and making sure their Christian record collection is as complete as required by their tastes. That is not what life is for.'[33]

Let's start again

Many people are sweepingly critical of today's youth. Even within the Christian church there are those who dismiss teenagers out of hand as being so completely caught up in 'doing their own thing' that they are not prepared to listen to a careful examination of issues such as rock music and the gospel. *We couldn't agree less.* As we have spoken to youth groups around the country while preparing the material for this book we have been very encouraged by the response. Some have been stunned; they had not realized that occultism and other evils had penetrated rock music so deeply; others had never given serious thought to the possibility that, regardless of the lyrics, the music itself is saying something; others have been challenged to

become more discriminating about their music. Others
have been prepared to go even further, to dismantle
their popular prejudices and to take a totally fresh look
at their whole approach to music — 'secular' and
'Christian' — based not on the pressures of a worldly
youth culture, but on the principles of the Word of
God. Our prayer is that this book will help many more
to do the same.

9.
Getting in tune with God

Jesus Christ has always had more fans than followers. Many people attracted by his personality, fascinated by his power or impressed by his teaching have never truly submitted to him as the Lord of their lives. This is not surprising. The reason most people do not become Christians is not because being a follower of Christ is too soft, but because it is too hard. There are many like the man who said, 'I will follow you, Lord; *but* . . .' (Luke 9:61); not so many prepared to fulfil the basic conditions for discipleship: 'If anyone comes to me and does not hate . . . even his own life – he cannot be my disciple' (Luke 14:26).

Those are not easy terms – but they are simple. Normal Christianity means obedience to Christ in every part of life, whatever the cost. It means setting aside one's own tastes and preferences, likes and dislikes, and submitting every area of life to this one crucial test: *what does Christ want me to do*? He himself put it like this: 'My sheep listen to my voice; I know them, and they follow me' (John 10:27). Nothing could be clearer. The two hallmarks of the Christian are determination to hear whatever God says and an equal determination to do whatever God commands – to have what Al Martin calls 'an open ear and an obedient foot'!

With that in mind, let us turn specifically to the question of 'Christian music' (which obviously includes the use of pop music in evangelism). What are some of the biblical principles that apply? Before answering that question, it goes without saying that *all* 'Christian music' must submit to the same principles. Personal taste is not the issue. A classical style must keep to the same rules as a contemporary one; the organ and the guitar must be treated alike; the robed choir must be assessed in the same way as the rock group. With that in mind, what principles should govern the music we use in God's service? Perhaps the best way to discover this is to allow us to ask you these questions about the music you write, play, sing, listen to, or use in worship or evangelism.

1. *Does it help you to hear the Word of God clearly?*
The Bible says that 'Faith comes from *hearing the message*, and the message is heard through the word of Christ' (Romans 10:17) and speaks about 'setting forth the truth *plainly*' (2 Corinthians 4:2). The first test is therefore whether the message can be heard — and this must be applied in at least three ways. The first has to do with the *sound* of the music, and with its relationship to the words. After all, it is obvious there is no gospel in the *music*. God gave us the gospel in *words* and nothing in the music must distort or blur or in any way push into the background what the Bible calls 'the word of truth, the gospel' (Colossians 1:5). If the volume or dissonance of the music are such that the words cannot be heard clearly, then the whole performance is an exercise in absurdity. Can we imagine playing loud or discordant music (or music of any kind) throughout a preacher's sermon in order to help to get the message across?

The test must also be applied in terms of the *character* of the composition. In John Calvin's words, 'We must beware . . . lest our ears be more intent on the music than our minds on the spiritual meaning of the words . . . Songs composed merely to tickle and delight the ear are unbecoming to the majesty of the church and cannot but be most displeasing to God.'[1] Strange as it may seem, it is possible for music to be *too good* to use in Christian worship, because it draws attention *from* the words instead of *to* them. Whatever its style or form, music must always be the servant of the Word of God, never its master. The great Augustine certainly recognized this. In his *Confessions* he wrote, 'I am inclined to approve the custom of singing in church. Nevertheless when it happens that I am more moved by the song than the thing which is sung, I confess that I sin in a manner deserving of punishment, and then I should rather not hear the singing.'[2]

Thirdly, the test must be applied to *the lyrics*. Do they help me to hear the Word of God? Some of our older hymns score heavily here, because they are no more than the Psalms or other parts of Scripture set to poetry and music. The same applies to some modern songs and choruses that have the same basis. But what about other songs? Are they Bible-based? Is the Word of God the thing that gets through? Is there solid doctrinal content? Not all hymnology is good theology. For an illustration of what we mean, we want to quote from *Background to the Task*, which was published in 1968 as a supplement to *On the Other Side*, a Report by the Evangelical Alliance Commission on Evangelism. In a section called 'Modern Music and Evangelism' Colin Chapman writes about some of the factors which make it difficult to use pop music to communicate the gospel and at one point mentions the difficulty of using an idiom in which 'love' plays such a large part. He then goes on to say this: 'If we are using an idiom or a medium which in the majority of cases is used to speak about some aspect of love, what effect is this likely to have on the content of the gospel song and

on the content of what actually comes across to the
listener? Could it be that in using this idiom we have
been unconsciously influenced by the associations of
the idiom, with the result that when we present Christ
in a gospel song we *appear* to be presenting him primarily as a kind of heavenly lover? Could it be that
what some of the audience hear is not so much a challenge to come to terms with the God who had made
them and to whom they are accountable for their
lives, but rather an invitation to fall in love with
Jesus? . . . But would we not be more faithful to the
gospel if we said that it is our refusal to love God
which constitutes the compelling need for us to come
to terms with God? . . .'[3] Chapman's questions still need
answering today and they point up one of the greatest
dangers in the pop gospel field. In an earlier chapter
we quoted two leading 'pop gospellers' admitting that
the content of most gospel pop songs today is doc-
trinally inadequate. If that is the case, they fail at the
first hurdle and we have no right to use them.

2. *Does this music tend to give you a greater vision of the glory of God?*

The first recorded song in Scripture is in Exodus 15 and
was sung by Moses and the Israelites to celebrate their
miraculous deliverance from the Egyptians. In it are
these remarkable words: 'The Lord is my strength and
my song; he has become my salvation' (Exodus 15:2).
What is remarkable about them is that Moses refers to
God as 'my song', and it would be impossible to link
the nature of God and the nature of the song more
closely than that! God not only caused the song, he
characterized it. No wonder Matthew Henry calls it
'a holy song, consecrated to the honour of God, and
intended to exalt his name and celebrate his praise,
and his only'.[4]

Can the same be said of your 'Christian music'? Accepting that its beat, rhythm and syncopations are saying things, are they things that express the purity, majesty, holiness and serenity of God? Music about God should be like God. It should reflect him, magnify him; it should communicate something of God's character. Does it do this? Is it pure in its tone, lovely in its melody? Fine-tuning the question to the subject of our study, does rock music do it?

The American evangelist David Wilkerson has had a remarkable ministry among drop-outs and other under-privileged young people and is very familiar with today's youth scene. How does he answer the question? In his book *Get your hands off my throat* he says this: 'Christian rock groups are brought to our youth cru-sades by sponsoring churches. They appear on my stage with their drums and loud guitars, hand clapping their way through songs that speak of Jesus, but with the primitive beat of rock. I try not to act surprised, offended or ashamed. You see, I want so much to relate to these young people. The kids in the audience seem to love every beat. They clap, they smile, they relate, they turn on and they get excited. But some-thing inside me, deep in my soul, does not feel right. There's a small hurt which I can't explain. I feel as though the Holy Spirit within me does not witness to the rock sounds in the middle of a salvation meet-ing. I also have a sense, an inner knowledge, that the gentle Holy Spirit is not comfortable in the atmosphere this music creates.'[5] Is Wilkerson right?

3. *Does this music tend to give you a repentant view of man's depravity?*

In describing man's spiritual state, the Bible says, 'The heart is deceitful above all things and beyond cure' (Jeremiah 17:9). One of man's most persistent follies

is to imagine that whenever he chooses he can pull
himself up by his spiritual bootlaces, turn to God, get
cleaned up, and become a member of God's family.
But that is not the case. Man is corrupt, vile, morally
and spiritually rotten to the core. Does your music
give you a *repentant* view of all this? The word in
italics is all-important. There is certainly a great deal
of music that gives a view of man's depravity. Rock
music's heavy emphasis on violence, anarchy, rebellion, sexual promiscuity, homosexuality, the drug
culture, blasphemy, occultism and the like is saying
something that is both loud and clear. One would
certainly hope that 'Christian music' would not glorify
those things, but neutrality is not enough. The questions we have to ask are these: does it lead you to search
your heart and not just to tap your feet? Does it get
beyond feelings to facts? Does it make clear to you the
reality of man's spiritual condition apart from God?

We have already suggested the great difficulties that
any idiom aimed at bringing pleasure has in conveying
the 'bad news' that it is vital for man to grasp before he
can appreciate the nature of the 'good news'. Does the
music you are playing, singing or hearing honestly over-
come all those difficulties and do it in such a way that
it helps to bring you to a place of repentance, a place
where you loathe sin and want to have nothing to do
with it?

4. *Does this kind of music encourage you to disciplined,*
   godly living?
Discovering the details of God's will for his life is the
constant concern of every serious-minded Christian, but
the overall will of God for him could not be clearer: 'It
is God's will that you should be holy' (1 Thessalonians
4:3). Yet holiness does not come easily; godliness is
never handed to the Christian on a plate. The Christian

life is a fight, not a festival; a conflict, not a concert. It is a constant battle against the forces of evil and calls for vigilance, discipline, sacrifice and spiritual determination. Does your music tend to lead you in these directions, or does it tend to be soft, slushy or sentimental? Does it help you to focus your mind on things that are 'true . . . noble . . . right . . . pure . . . lovely . . . admirable . . . and praiseworthy' (Philippians 4:8)? Even more importantly, does the music itself and the way it is performed enable you to focus your attention on *God* and not on the performers?

5. *Does this kind of music help you to separate yourself from the world?*

The Bible could not be clearer on the Christian's duty here: 'Do not love the world or anything in the world. If anyone loves the world, the love of the Father is not in him' (1 John 2:15). That has always been a tall order and perhaps never taller than in this day and age. Christians are under siege, pressurized day after day to conform to philosophies, values, standards and life-styles diametrically opposed to those laid down in Scripture, where we are told that 'God did not call us to be impure but to live a holy life' (1 Thessalonians 4:7) and that as far as these things are concerned we are to 'come out from them and be separate' (2 Corinthians 6:17). Yet in his book *Anatomy of Pop*, Roy Connolly adds this comment to the many we have quoted concerning pop music's ethos: 'The notes are only a gateway to a kind of physical and psychological freedom which human beings find necessary for their survival and sanity. The music is more at home in the club, the pub and the brothel, in close association with other group entertainment, drinking and seduction.'[6]

What voice are you hearing in your music? Does it appeal to the sensual or to the spiritual? Does it seem

to have its roots in this world or in heaven? Does it
stimulate pure appetites or impure? Does it lead you
to want more of the world's values, or less? Are godless people comfortable with it or embarrassed by it?
Does it help or hinder a desire to break free from the
worldly way of doing things? There is no neutrality
here — the Bible makes it clear that 'Anyone who
chooses to be a friend of the world becomes an enemy
of God' (James 4:4). The question is not essentially
one of what you like, but of whom you love.

6. *Is this the kind of music that you can imagine being part of a spiritual revival?*

This is a good test, because revival is a time when God
himself breaks through in breath-taking power and
glory — and therefore a time when we should expect
to see an emphasis on those things which have his
blessing. The psalmist prayed, 'Will you not revive us
again, that your people may rejoice in you?' (Psalm
85:6) — a reminder that revival is sent from God, not
staged by man.

What part does music have in such a movement? It
has been suggested that music is always strongly associated with every genuine revival, but while this may
have an element of truth in it, it certainly needs to be
heavily qualified. For example, in genuine revival music
is never prominent as a *performance*. There is certainly
congregational singing as God's people rejoice in the
Lord, but we are not aware of *any* genuine revival that
has centred around a musical 'star'. Surely that is
significant?

Wales has had a revival in each of the last three centuries — in 1735, 1859 and 1904. Yet although there
were claims of 100,000 conversions at the time, the
long-term results of the 1904 revival were comparatively
disappointing. For example, it is said that there were

2,000 conversions on Anglesey alone, yet a generation later the island was virtually a spiritual wilderness. Writing in *Reformation Today*, Gwynne Williams suggests some of the reasons for a lack of depth in the work associated with Evan Roberts (the leading preacher of the revival) and says there came a point when he and many of his followers 'lost touch with the essential sanity of New Testament Christianity. Human techniques were used to build up an atmosphere of expectancy; repetitive prayer or *the studied use of music* were especially to the fore.'[7] He then describes his own great-grandfather telling how 'hymns and solos were carefully arranged so as to provide the revivalist with an audience which had been emotionally moved' and adds, 'Incidentally these were the first real examples of entertainment evangelism in Wales, Roberts himself being almost always accompanied by musicians.'[8]

That is a fascinating glimpse into the church's history, but it is more than that. It has often been said that those who will not learn from history are doomed to repeat its mistakes, and the lessons from 1904 can begin to be learned by asking ourselves some questions. Is this music God-centred or man-centred? Does it concentrate on the Lord's glory or on man's feelings? Does it draw attention to the performers or to Christ? Whenever music makes it difficult to see the Son for the stars, we can be sure that there is something wrong!

7. *Is this the kind of music under whose influence you can imagine Christians drawn into sacrificial full-time missionary service?*
Christ's final command to his disciples was to 'go into all the world and preach the good news to all creation' (Mark 16:15), and it has been said that one of the marks of a church's spiritual health is the measure in which it

takes its share in the fulfilment of that commission. It
is usually a good sign when a church can point to a
steady stream of young people and others who have
left the security and comfort of job and home and
obeyed God's call to full-time missionary service regardless of the cost, and usually a bad sign when a church
has to delve back many years to find the last person
who did so. Does this have anything to do with young
people's pre-occupation with a certain kind of music?
Not necessarily, but we feel that some honest questions
might be helpful. Does this kind of music appeal to
sentiment, or does it touch you at a deeper level?
Does it merely encourage enjoyment, or does it lead to
evangelism? Does it call you to indulgence, or to sacrifice? Is it music which helps you thoughtfully to count
the cost of whole-hearted commitment to Christ? The
questions are valid — and the answers revealing! Perhaps
a subsidiary question will help to test where your
priorities really lie: how does the amount you give
directly to missionary work compare with what you
spend on your music?

8. *Would you expect to find this kind of music in heaven?*

Earlier in this book we quoted Martin Luther as saying
that the man who did not appreciate music was 'a clod'.
We can go further than that and say that the Christian
who does not appreciate music is almost a contradiction,
because he is on his way to a place where he will be
surrounded by music for all eternity! One of the things
revealed by God to the apostle John during his remarkable vision on the island of Patmos was that *there will
be music in heaven*. In one of the most breath-taking
passages in all Scripture we are told about three tremendous songs of praise. The first is where 'four living
creatures and the twenty-four elders . . . sang a new

song' (Revelation 5:8, 9). Then we are told that 'Many angels, numbering thousands upon thousands, and ten thousand times ten thousand . . . encircled the throne and . . . sang' (Revelation 5:11–12). Finally John tells us, 'I heard every creature in heaven and on earth and under the earth and on the sea, and all that is in them, singing: "To him who sits on the throne and to the Lamb be praise and honour and glory and power, for ever and ever!"' (Revelation 5:13.)

The first choir has twenty-eight members — four 'living creatures' and twenty-four elders (representing nature and the church?); then they are joined by at least 104 million angels (work it out!); finally by every creature in the entire universe. No wonder Christina Rossetti once described heaven as the homeland of music! But what kind of music is it? Is it music as we know it, with staves and scales, chords and canons? Will there be melody, harmony and rhythm as we know them here? We have no idea. We are not given any details about the music — perhaps to enable us to concentrate on the words. It will certainly be 'a new song' (Revelation 5:9), but as William Freel has said, 'No composer can estimate its value, no instrument can play its harmony, no voice can pronounce its beauty, no modulator can convey its height or its depth; *this song is arranged to please the ear of God*.'[9]

That immediately points us to some important and inescapable questions. Does the music you enjoy suggest that it was arranged for the same ear? Can you imagine it being enjoyed by God the Father? Is it *serious* music? Does it promote a sense of awe and reverence? Can you imagine it being enjoyed by God the Son? Does it give undivided glory to 'the Lamb, who was slain'? (Revelation 5:12.) Can you imagine it being enjoyed by God the Holy Spirit? Does it speak of peace, purity and a spirit of worship? There are other questions to be asked, too. Can you imagine this music being played and sung by the angels and archangels, the cherubim and seraphim? Perhaps even more testing is this: can you imagine that when you get to heaven and stand before the indescribable majesty of the triune God of glory this is the kind of music you will want to play and the kind of song you will want to sing?

The apostle Paul says of Christians that 'our citizenship is in heaven' (Philippians 3:20). That being so, every part of life should be seen as a preparation for that glorious experience. Our music is no exception.

10.
Back to square one

The story is told of a man who, during an election campaign, had a bumper sticker on his car which read, 'My mind is made up — don't confuse me with the facts.' The story has whiskers but it is relevant. As we have seen, the subject of rock or pop music in evangelism is wide-ranging and complicated, but that has not prevented a great many people (young and old) jumping in at the deep end and delivering their first and last words on the subject without giving it the amount of serious, *honest* thought it demands.

Throughout this book we have tried to be both serious and honest, and to examine the whole subject carefully and courteously, listening to what the experts have to say and keeping personal preferences out of the discussion altogether. We hope we have succeeded, but we would be wrong to leave the whole thing up in the air. Discussion must be followed by direction and decision.

All you have to do . . .

One of the most unusual books in the Bible is Ecclesiastes. Written by an anonymous author known only as 'the Teacher', it is a remarkable commentary on human life and on man's relationship with God. On the last page, we read these words: 'Now all has been heard; here is the conclusion of the matter: Fear God

and keep his commandments, for this is the whole duty
of man' (Ecclesiastes 12:13). Of course the 'Teacher' is
right. When all is said and done, man's whole duty consists in fearing (worshipping) God and being obedient
to his Word. Someone has said that loving God is reading
the Bible and doing what it says, and no Christian
should disagree with that. Yet as far as pop music and
evangelism are concerned, that statement makes the
issue both clear and unclear! It makes it clear in that all
that is required is obedience: cultural differences,
personal preferences and human opinions are irrelevant.
It makes it unclear in that the Bible makes no mention
of pop music in evangelism. Where do we go from there?

In his excellent book *Nothing but the Truth*, Brian
Edwards has a chapter entitled 'The Bible, sufficient and
final' in which he says this: 'All matters of doctrine and
life are to be brought to the final test of Scripture.
There are no subjects upon which Scripture has nothing
to say either by *direct command* or *indirect principle* —
this is what is meant by the sufficiency of Scripture.'[1]
As far as pop music in evangelism is concerned, there
are obviously no *commands* in the Bible. In fact, as we
saw in an earlier chapter, there are no directions about
the use of *any* kind of music in evangelism. It is neither
commanded nor commended; there is no example of its
being used; it is not even hinted at — and for many
Christians past and present that is where the discussion
begins and ends. All the arguments we have brought to
bear in this book would be considered irrelevant. They
would go along with the Puritan preacher John Trapp
in saying, 'Where Scripture hath no tongue, we must
have no ears,' and that is a perfectly honourable position
to take. Many of the historic doctrinal confessions
which surrounded the Reformation did exactly this. The
Heidelberg Catechism (1563) said that we were not to
worship God 'in any other way than he has commanded

in his Word'. The Belgic Confession (1566) said that the Scriptures 'fully contain the will of God . . . The whole manner of worship God requires of us is written in them'. The Westminster Confession of Faith (1646) said, 'The acceptable way of worshipping the true God is instituted by himself' and that God may not be worshipped according to 'the imaginations and devices of men . . . or in any other way not prescribed in the Holy Scripture'. The Baptist Confession of Faith (1689) said that 'The only acceptable way of worshipping the true God is appointed by himself in accordance with his own will . . . and all other forms of worship not prescribed in Holy Scripture are expressly forbidden.' Whatever else may be thought, these statements were not drawn up by extremists or cranks, but by our fathers in the faith, those to whom, under God, we owe our Christian heritage today.

If this is your position, reading this book has been purely academic; the silence of Scripture had already convinced you that there is no biblical place for music in evangelism. However, it must be said that a rigid application of this rule (what theologians call 'the regulative principle') does raise massive difficulties in its application to other areas of church life. It buries the 'music in evangelism' issue, but a hundred problems grow on the grave. As we cannot possibly touch on these here, let us turn to the other way of applying the Bible's teaching.

The point about principles

What is the difference between a biblical command and a biblical principle? Brian Edwards gives a clear and simple illustration in his book. A church which keeps a register of its members is doing something not commanded in

Scripture; but there is a biblical *principle* which says
that things should be done 'in a fitting and orderly
way' (1 Corinthians 14:40), which makes a list of
church members sensible and practical. On the other
hand, a church which made a charge for membership
would be violating a biblical principle; the Bible says
that a Christian's giving should be 'in keeping with
his income' (1 Corinthians 16:2), and not according to
a scale of fees laid down by the church.[2]

How does this apply to pop gospel evangelism? In
the course of this book we have sought to bring biblical
principles to bear on the subject at every stage: in
evangelism, words are of paramount importance;
nothing must detract or distract from them in any way;
any kind of psychological manipulation must be
avoided; nothing must be done that will stimulate un-
wholesome thoughts or appetites; the message must be
addressed directly to the mind and not merely to the
emotions; the communicator must do everything he
can to be obliterated by the message; the message must
tell the 'bad news' as well as the 'good news'; the
message must be communicated seriously, earnestly,
urgently — and so on. *It is our conviction that entertainment evangelism fails to meet these and other
biblical principles and is therefore contrary to the
teaching of Scripture and should be abandoned.*

The law of liberty

Although we have tried to present the issue fairly and
positively, that last paragraph will sound to some like
a prison sentence — harsh, cramping, negative, destructive. Yet if it is biblically sound, that cannot be
the case. James calls Scripture 'the law that gives freedom' (James 2:12), while one of the psalmists says,

'I will walk about in freedom, for I have sought out your precepts' (Psalm 119:45). In a nutshell, this means that *the person who is tied to Scripture is set free from everything else* and this emancipation is part of what Paul calls 'the glorious freedom of the children of God' (Romans 8:21). How does this apply to our conclusions? What kind of freedom do you have if you decide to abandon entertainment evangelism? The difficulty in answering the question is not in knowing where to start, but in knowing when to stop.

In the first place, you are free from tradition. It is only in the last hundred years or so that musical evangelism has become a tradition, and in the last twenty-five years that pop gospel has become a tradition within a tradition. Yet you are not bound by either. You have discovered that Christians are called to be true radicals — always linking back to the roots instead of getting caught up in the branches!

On the other hand, you are free from needing to keep in step with the latest style and idiom of gospel presentation. You do not have to be musically 'with it'. You are also free from the risk of turning people away from the gospel because they do not like the style or quality of your music. Recently, Christians at a university told us of some Muslims they had persuaded to attend an evangelistic rally, but had difficulty getting them to stay long enough to hear the evangelist. The reason was the rock music played in the early part of the meeting, which seemed to confirm their worst fears — that Christianity was a Western religion with no message for them.

The Bible asks, 'Who can bring what is pure from the impure?' (Job 14:4), but you have been set free from the need to try to wrench your evangelistic music away from its grubby associations — rebelliousness, occultism, sexuality, the drug culture and the like.

Christian pop artists invariably imitate the clothing, gestures, movements and voices of secular performers; the whole style is set by the world — but you have been set free from the danger of gospel rock presentations creating or stimulating an appetite for the same kind of music outside of a Christian framework.

You are free from all the dangers associated with psychological manipulation in gospel pop, as well as from the dangers of an emotional response based on the beat, rhythm and pulse of the music rather than on the words. You are also free from the serious consequences of evacuating the message in order to accommodate the music and from the trivializing of truth which results from trying to reduce great doctrines to 'pop words'.

In addition, you are free from the twin dangers associated with the quality of the music — that either the music is so good or so powerful that it overwhelms the words, or so poor that the words are condemned along with the performance.

You are free from the temptation of relying on the music to 'get results'. A youth group recently pleaded with us to include a rock band in an evangelistic mission because 'if we get a band it will make it easier for people to get saved'. Our answer was to say, 'That depends on who does the saving!' There was no band (rock or otherwise) on the day of Pentecost when 3,000 were converted, nor in the amazing days which followed, when '*the Lord* added to [the church] daily those who were being saved' (Acts 2:47). You will obviously long for God to use your evangelistic efforts to bring people to himself, but you are free to place your unqualified obedience to his Word above any pressure to produce immediate results.

Finally, and by no means unimportantly, you are free from the embarrassment of needing to explain why so soon after a large number of 'decisions' are recorded, there is so little lasting effect to be seen in the lives of many of those concerned.

The other side of freedom

All the freedoms we have mentioned so far might be called 'negative freedoms': they refer to areas of danger and difficulty from which you are delivered by abandoning entertainment evangelism. But there is another side to freedom. When a person manages to escape through the Iron Curtain he is not only set free *from* Eastern Europe but *into* Western Europe. By abandoning entertainment evangelism you are not only free *from* certain areas, you are also set free *into* other areas.

In the first place, you are free to concentrate much more (as speaker or listener) on *the preaching of the Word of God*. Many Christians have either forgotten or failed to notice the central place that God has given to preaching in the work of evangelism. John the Baptist prepared the way for the coming of Jesus by '*preaching* in the Desert of Judea' (Matthew 3:1). As soon as Jesus began his public ministry he 'began to *preach*' (Matthew 4:17). His final command to his disciples was 'Go into all the world and *preach* the good news to all creation' (Mark 16:15). As a result, we read that 'Day after day, in the temple courts and from house to house, they never stopped *teaching and proclaiming* the good news that Jesus is the Christ' (Acts 5:42). When persecution drove the 'ordinary' church members out of Jerusalem, 'Those who had been scattered *preached* the word wherever they went' (Acts 8:4). Paul was crystal clear about his own commission: 'For Christ did not send me to baptize, but to *preach* the gospel' (1 Corinthians 1:17). He told Titus that God had 'brought his word to

light through the *preaching* entrusted to me by the
command of God our Saviour' (Titus 1:3). Having
rejoiced that 'everyone who calls on the name of the
Lord will be saved' (Romans 10:13), he went on to
ask these questions: 'How, then, can they call on the
one they have not believed in? And how can they
believe in the one of whom they have not heard? And
how can they hear without someone *preaching* to them?'
(Romans 10:14). In a very telling comment on all this,
Geoffrey Wilson says, 'The apostles constantly laboured
to inform the minds of their hearers. They did not
exercise a commission to pander to the basest instincts
of the natural man.'[3]

We have lost that emphasis today. As Paul Bassett
rightly says, 'We sing of Christ, recite Christ, dramatize
Christ, but less and less do we preach Christ.'[4] We
have reached the extraordinary situation where the
evangelist has to fight for his place on the evangelistic
platform. He is becoming an endangered species! It
would not be an exaggeration to say that musical evangelism has become an obsession for many of those
involved in youth evangelism in Britain today. Many
would not consider the possibility of a major evangelistic effort without employing a band as the central
feature. In a very real sense, the medium has become
the message. Surely it is time to turn the tide? In recent
missions we have been very encouraged by the attendance, attention and response at meetings which concentrated almost exclusively on the preaching of the gospel.
We believe that it is time for those in positions of
responsibility to do some serious, biblical rethinking in
this area. The Bible tells us that when Christ ascended
into heaven he made full provision for the ongoing work
of the kingdom of God by bestowing various gifts on
the church: 'some to be apostles, some to be prophets,
some to be evangelists, and some to be pastors and

teachers . . .' (Ephesians 4:11). Is there no significance in the fact that he did not include entertainers in the list?

Yet some people in the pop gospel world even suggest that music is a better medium than words for the communication of the gospel. In a letter from which he has given us permission to quote, Robert Andrews of Chapel Lane Productions says that in certain situations 'when we choose to preach to them using words only, the level of communication is minimal'. Another Christian heavily involved in contemporary Christian music went so far as to say, 'If it is "impossible to communicate the gospel of Romans in music, drama or dance", it is even more impossible for preachers, whose words can go nowhere as far to communicate the depth of the concepts involved.' We wonder what comment that might have produced from Dr Martyn Lloyd-Jones, who managed to keep going through Romans at Westminster Chapel on Friday nights for thirteen years, from 1955–1968, without needing a single note of music to communicate 'the depth of the concepts involved'!

Even more importantly, that philosophy fails to grasp the tremendous truth that preaching cannot be divorced from the gospel. The method and the message are inseparable – and *non-verbal communication does not count as preaching*. To give an obvious example: Paul told the Corinthians, 'For Christ did not send me to baptize, but to preach the gospel' (1 Corinthians 1:17). Baptism is obviously a valid form of communication – one that is biblical and God-ordained – but Paul's point is that it is quite distinct from the preaching of the gospel. Baptism is good, right and biblical, but it is not preaching.

The point becomes even clearer when we take a closer look at Paul's phrase, 'to preach the gospel'. In the original Greek this is just one word – *euangeliseathai,* which we sometimes transliterate 'to evangelize'. But the word Paul uses is a verbal form of the noun *euangelion* — and we would be more strictly accurate to translate his statement: 'Christ did not send me to baptize, but to *gospel*.' The gospel and the preaching of the gospel are as closely linked as that. A little further on in his letter, Paul says that people would have preferred some other form of communication: 'Jews demand miraculous signs and Greeks look for wisdom' (1 Corinthians 1:22). What was Paul's response? God had used him to perform miracles before; why not ask for power to perform more? He certainly had the intellectual capacity to tangle with the Greeks at a rational and philosophical level; why not try to win them over that way? Yet Paul's response was to satisfy neither group. He knew of only one way to meet their need: 'We *preach* Christ crucified' (1 Corinthians 1:23). As far as Paul was concerned, nothing else could properly communicate the gospel, not even the powerful alternatives suggested by some. *If preaching cannot be replaced by miracles, how can it possibly be replaced by music?*

Secondly — and this applies especially to young Christians — you are free to get more closely involved *in the work, worship and fellowship of your local church.* There is no doubt that when young people are heavily involved in the pop gospel scene they tend to drift away from the basic life of the local church. Our experience in countless churches would bear this out almost to the extent that we see a kind of sliding-scale operating. The farther young people are into musical evangelism, the less they tend to support the vital structures of the church, and vice-versa. When music takes over, corporate prayer and Bible study, church involvement and missionary interest (other than the sensational or unusual) decline. A prayer meeting or Bible study probably seems pretty tame after a gospel concert! Even Sunday attendance suffers: we know of young people who will go by the coachload to a gospel concert on a Saturday night, then miss Sunday morning's service. Youth leaders have a particular responsibility here, by example, by encouragement and by the planning of programmes that will help to steer young people in the right direction.

Thirdly, you are free to concentrate on what are clearly *New Testament methods of evangelism.* What are they? Writing in *Evangelical Times,* Geoff. Thomas suggested that 'The only New Testament precedents for spreading the gospel are godly living, praying and bold speaking.'[5] That sounds pretty meagre, but it is far from it, because the 'bold speaking' covers an almost endless variety of things. 'Bold speaking' can obviously take place in a pulpit or on a platform, but it can also take place at informal church-based functions or on neutral ground; it can take place at home or at work, at a social or sports club, at school, college or university, in a car, a 'bus, a train or an aircraft – in fact wherever two or more people get into conversation. In an Eastern European country recently, church leaders told us that at one stage they had become discouraged at not being able to use many of the evangelistic methods available to us in the West. Then they had second thoughts and decided that they were wrong to feel like that, because they could use all the methods available to the church in the New Testament! As Geoff. Thomas adds in his article, 'What turned the world upside down then is sufficient to do it today.'[6] Time saved in advertising, planning, organizing, supporting and attending gospel concerts, religious road shows and the like can be put to better use in activities that have clear New Testament backing.

Fourthly, you are free to spend more time in *personal evangelism.* There is a case for saying that this was the most widely used method of evangelism in the New Testament, and another for saying that it is the most widely neglected in the church today. In his racy paperback *Evangelism – Now and Then*, Michael Green comments, 'This is the biggest difference between the New Testament church and our own. Their responsibility of bearing witness to Jesus rested fairly and squarely upon every single member . . . These days evangelism is spasmodic (if it happens at all), expensive . . . and is dependent upon the skills of the resident evangelist or visiting specialist. This is exceedingly foolish.'[7] One of the reasons it is foolish is that it limits the greatest task in the world to the efforts of a tiny minority of Christians and to a very small fraction of their time. In the business world, that kind of policy would be a recipe for bankruptcy. In a famous report published by the Church of England in 1945 under the title *Towards the Conversion of England*, it was said that 'There will be no widespread evangelization of England unless the work is undertaken by the lay people of the church.'[8] That statement remains true today.

It also helps to pinpoint one of the weaknesses of 'gospel rock' and that is that its 'target area' is so limited. In a nutshell, it is juvenile, appealing almost exclusively to the young. It has little to say to the mature and middle-aged and nothing at all to the elderly, the sick, the dying, or the millions who are turned off by its very style. What is more, there are scores of situations in which it is totally out of place – a house meeting, a funeral, a classroom, a hospital ward, and so on.

On the other hand, verbal communication is relevant to every person, in every place and at any time. There is no situation in which the spoken word may not be an effective vehicle for communicating the gospel, for the simple reason that it is the method God ordained for the purpose.

One of the most exciting things about personal evangelism is that it is something open to every Christian. Have you ever thought of the wisdom of God in this? You do not have to be musical or theatrical, gifted or extrovert, nor do you have to gather an audience or advertise your ability. Going back to Geoff. Thomas's three New Testament methods, every Christian can pray, every Christian is called to live a godly life and every Christian can speak about Christ. In his infinite love and wisdom, God has put the greatest privilege in the world within the reach of every Christian believer!

But realistic and consistent personal evangelism takes time. It means building bridges of personal friendship, investing in people's lives as well as their souls. It means getting to grips with their personal situations, trying to think through their problems, patiently seeking to answer their questions. Personal evangelism is not a hit-and-run affair, nor is it realistically done merely by taking someone along to an evangelistic event of some kind.

Fifthly, you are free to invest more time in *Bible study and prayer*. This is not a change of subject! The key to effective personal witnessing for Christ (and to effective Christian living as a whole) is not to be found in frantic activity, but in the Christian's personal relationship with the Lord. Moving in exciting circles is not the same as getting somewhere! This instruction from the apostle Peter points us in the right direction here: 'But in your hearts set apart Christ as Lord. Always be prepared to give an answer to everyone who asks you to give the reason for the hope that you have' (1 Peter 3:15). But how can a Christian possibly 'be prepared to give an answer' unless he knows what the answer is? Having a copy of the latest translation of the

Bible is no substitute for knowing what it says — and our observations would lead us to believe that many young Christians' preoccupation with gospel music (listening, reading, discussing, attending and so on) has been a major factor in reducing the amount of time available to invest in deepening their own spiritual lives by determined Bible study and effective prayer. The loss to the church — and therefore to the kingdom of God — has been incalculable.

The urgent need of the hour is for a generation of Christian young people who are spiritual giants, sold out to God and determined 'to say "No" to ungodliness and worldly passions, and to live self-controlled, upright and godly lives in this present age' (Titus 2:12). Anything that even *tends* to cool that kind of determination marks a point of spiritual tragedy in the life of the person concerned.

Decision time

In writing this book we believe that we have discharged an important responsibility; now the responsibility shifts from author to reader. We have tried to work through the issue thoroughly, carefully and honestly, without at any point being destructively critical of Christians who might not agree with us. We sincerely believe that the case against the use of pop music in evangelism is overwhelming, but we recognize, of course, that our convictions are not binding on others. Our final direction would therefore come straight from Scripture: 'Each one should be fully convinced in his own mind' (Romans 14:5).

The issue with which Paul was dealing at the time (the religious observance of certain days in the Jewish calendar) was not as important as the present one, but his words are powerfully relevant and pinpoint two vital principles. The first two words — 'each one' — emphasize your *liberty*, the birthright of every Christian. You have no reason to be browbeaten by anyone, nor do you have any need to go along with the crowd. The matter under discussion is one between you and God and you have the right and the privilege of exercising your own conscience in the light of the Word of God. Never let the fact that many or even most Christians take a certain line on a particular issue rob you of your own God-given prerogative.

The second principle is that of your *responsibility:* Paul says that a Christian should be 'fully convinced in his own mind'. The phrase 'fully convinced' is one you would use about gathering evidence and also carries with it the sense of being filled to the brim. Bring these two strands of thought together, recognize that this is not just a suggestion but a command, and you have a picture of just how great a responsibility you have. The issue of entertainment evangelism is tremendously important, not least because evangelism is a matter of life and death. It is seeking to rescue those who are 'without hope and without God in the world' (Ephesians 2:12). The question of how the rescue operation should be carried out is not, therefore, something on which vague ideas will do — and to have a 'couldn't care less' attitude is downright carnal. Here is something about which you have a responsibility to be 'fully convinced' — up to the brim! You must weigh up all the evidence and think carefully and honestly about all the arguments brought forward. At the same time, you must set aside your own emotions, tastes, likings and prejudices: in coming to a biblical conclusion these are irrelevant.

You have a right to your own judgement on the issue, but as a Christian you have a responsibility to base that judgement solely on the commands and principles of Scripture. In other words, what you think must be controlled by what God says.

At the beginning of the year in which he died, the missionary Spencer Walton wrote these words in his diary: 'The will of God — nothing less — nothing more — nothing else.' On the issue of entertainment evangelism, as on every other issue, that should be all you want to know and all you want to do.

References

Chapter 1
1. M. Doney, *Summer in the City*
2. As above
3. S. Lawhead, *Rock Reconsidered*
4. As above
5. J. Van Zyl, *Reformation Today*
6. R. Gruver, *Down Beat*
7. M. Doney, *Summer in the City*
8. B. Larson, *Rock*
9. M. Doney, *Summer in the City*
10. As above
11. S. Lawhead, *Rock Reconsidered*
12. M. Doney, *Summer in the City*
13. N. Cohn, *WopBopaLooBopLop-BamBoom*
14. D. Jewell, *The Popular Voice*
15. M. Doney, *Summer in the City*
16. D. Jewell, *The Popular Voice*
17. As above
18. S. Lawhead, *Rock Reconsidered*

Chapter 2
1. S. Lawhead, *Rock Reconsidered*
2. D. Jewell, *The Popular Voice*
3. W. Shafer, *Rock Music*
4. A. Salter, *What is Hypnosis?*
5. *Life*, 3.10.69
6. B. Larson, *The Day Music Died*
7. I. Stravinsky and R. Craft, *Horizon*, Sept. '58
8. B. Larson, *The Day Music Died*
9. T. McSloy, *National Review*, 30.6.70
10. D. M. Lloyd-Jones, *Preaching and Preachers*
11. D. Winter, *New Singer, New Song*
12. D. M. Lloyd-Jones, *Preaching and Preachers*
13. D. Jewell, *The Popular Voice*
14. M. Doney, *Summer in the City*
15. As above
16. D. Hanson and R. Fearn, *The Lancet*, 2.8.75
17. W. Burns and D. Robinson, *Hearing and Noise in Industry*
18. *The Lancet*, 2.8.75
19. As above
20. As above
21. H. Rookmaker, *The Creative Gift*

Chapter 3
1. *The Sunday Telegraph*, 5.9.82
2. As above
3. S. Lawhead, *Rock Reconsidered*
4. *U.S. News and World Report*, 31.10.77
5. *Planet*, Oct. '71
6. L. Roxon, *Rock Encyclopaedia*
7. B. Larson, *Rock*
8. *Rolling Stone*, 22.7.71
9. *Rolling Stone*, 25.3.76
10. *Daily Express*, 22.12.81
11. *Newsweek*, 21.12.81
12. B. Larson, *Rock*
13. *Circus*, April '74
14. B. Larson, *Rock*
15. *Daily Mirror*, 24.11.81
16. T. Palmer, *Born under a Bad Sign*
17. S. Lawhead, *Rock Reconsidered*
18. As above
19. M. Doney, *Summer in the City*
20. As above
21. *Rolling Stone*, 7.10.76
22. *Rolling Stone*, 9.2.78
23. B. Larson, *Rock*
24. *Billboard*, 11.12.76
25. *People*, 30.6.75
26. *Hit Parader*, Sept. '79
27. *Detroit News*, 7.7.67
28. *Newsweek*, 4.1.71

29. *Rolling Stone*, 17.7.75
30. *Rolling Stone*, 12.11.70
31. *Circus*, 17.10.78
32. *Fort Lauderdale News*, 6.3.69
33. *Circus*, 31.1.76
34. *Rolling Stone*, 7.1.71
35. *Circus*, 23.6.77
36. *People*, 21.5.79
37. *Life*, 28.6.68
38. *Time*, 3.1.69
39. *Newsweek*, 2.4.79
40. *Daily Mirror*, 18.11.81
41. *Daily Mail*, 21.1.83
42. *Daily Mail*, 18.3.83
43. G. Melly, *Revolt into Style*
44. As above
45. *Daily Telegraph*, 23.9.81
46. S. Lawhead, *Rock Reconsidered*
47. R.Taylor, *A Return to Christian Culture*
48. *Buzz*, Feb. '83
49. As above
50. B. Larson, *The Day Music Died*

Chapter 4

1. B. Larson, *Rock and the Church*
2. L. Morris, *New Bible Dictionary*
3. P. Anderson, *Talk of the Devil*
4. *Buzz*, April '82.
5. As above
6. *Hit Parader*, Nov. '68
7. B. Larson, *Rock*
8. *Rolling Stone*, 16.3.72
9. *Circus*, Dec. '71
10. *Rolling Stone*, 28.10.71
11. *Circus*, Feb. '76
12. *Hit Parader*, Feb. '78
13. *Newsweek*, 24.8.81
14. *Rolling Stone*, 12.2.76
15. *Hit Parader*, July '75
16. *Time*, 15.8.75
17. *Circus*, 19.1.77
18. *Newsweek*, 10.5.76
19. This group is in no way connected with the group 'Genesis' who appear on the Pilgrim label.
20. *Rolling Stone*, 26.10.72
21. B. Larson, *The Day Music Died*
22. Quoted in *Buzz*, May '82
23. *Circus*, 12.10.76
24. *Rolling Stone*, 20.3.72
25. *Newsweek*, 27.3.72

26. *Time*, 11.9.78
27. *Rolling Stone*, 1.7.76
28. *Circus*, 16.8.76
29. *Rolling Stone*, 19.8.71
30. *Newsweek*, 4.1.71
31. *Rolling Stone*, 16.12.76
32. *Hit Parader*, 4.12.78
33. *Buzz*, April '82
34. *Circus*, Nov. '74
35. *Billboard*, 10.12.77
36. *Buzz*, April '82
37. T. Palmer, *Born under a Bad Sign*
38. *People*, 19.7.76
39. B. Larson, *Rock*
40. *Buzz*, Feb. '83
41. *Youth Aflame*, Oct. '82
42. As above
43. *Time*, 31.10.69
44. *Circus*, 22.12.77
45. *Rolling Stone*, 12.2.76
46. M. Jones, *Rock Quotes*
47. B. Larson, *The Day Music Died*
48. *Time*, 14.3.83
49. As above
50. B. Larson, *Rock and the Church*
51. *Buzz*, Feb. '83
52. *Buzz*, April '82
53. B. Larson, *Rock*

Chapter 5

1. *Time*, 22.9.67
2. D. Pichaske, *A Generation in Motion*
3. *Toronto Daily Star*, 20.6.70
4. *Circus*, 17.4.79
5. As above
6. *Reader's Digest*, Dec. '69
7. *Young Life*, Vol. 56, No. 2
8. M. Doney, *Summer in the City*
9. *Circus*, 13.5.70
10. G. Melly, *Revolt into Style*
11. *The Listener*, 11.2.82
12. *Saturday Evening Post*, 8-15.8.64
13. J. Lennon, *A Spaniard in the Works*
14. *Hit Parader*, 19.6.75
15. *Time*, 9.11.70
16. *Newsweek*, 9.7.73
17. B. Larson, *Rock and the Church*
18. Appendix to *Time to Listen, Time to Talk* (J. & M. Prince)
19. *Leicester Mercury*, 4.1.82

20. D. Beaumont, *New Life* (Australia

21. *Leicester Mercury*, 4.1.82
22. B. Larson, *Rock*
23. *Buzz*, April '82
24. As above
25. D. Porter, *Media*
26. Quoted in *Time to Listen, Time to Talk* (J. & M. Prince)
27. *Reader's Digest*, Feb. '70
28. As above
29. Quoted in *Contemporary Christian Music*, Aug.–Sept. '81
30. As above
31. C. Scott, *Music: its secret influence through the ages*
32. *Daily Mirror*, 2.1.82
33. *Reading Chronicle*, 5.11.82
34. *Circus*, 13.5.76
35. K. Green, *Can God use Rock Music?*
36. W. Shafer, *Rock Music*
37. S. Ostrander and L. Schroeder, *Super Learning*
38. As above
39. I.K.Taimni, *The Science of Yoga*
40. W.B.Key, *Subliminal Seduction*
41. T.Leary, *Politics of Ecstasy*
42. *Hit Parader Yearbook*, No.6, '67
43. *Star Weekly Magazine*, 26.8.67
44. *Hit Parader*, Jan. '68
45. *Melody Maker*, 7.10.67
46. *The Guardian*, 28.12.82
47. W. B. Key, *The Clam-bake Orgy*
48. W.B.Key, *Subliminal Seduction*

Chapter 6

1. Quoted by C. Barnes, *God's Army*
2. *Evangelism Today*, Dec. '81
3. T. Morton, *Christian Graduate*, Mar. '81
4. T. Morton, *Solid Rock?*
5. J. Allen, *Solid Rock?*
6. A. W. Tozer, *Man: the Dwelling Place of God*
7. P. Bassett, *God's Way*
8. D. Hesselgrave, *Communicating Christ Cross-Culturally*
9. G. Gray, Appendix to *Time to Listen, Time to Talk* (J&M Prince)
10. L. Norman, *Solid Rock?*

11. As above
12. J. Fischer, *Solid Rock?*
13. *Chambers' Twentieth Century Dictionary*
14. As above
15. Plato, *Fourth Book of the Republic*
16. Boethius, *De Institutione Musica*
17. J. Calvin, *Works*, Vol. VI
18. S. Ostrander and L. Schroeder, *Super Learning*
19. C. Scott, *Music: Its secret influence through the ages*
20. G. Stevenson, *Music and your Emotions*
21. H. Hanson, *American Journal of Psychiatry*
22. B. Larson, *The Day Music Died*
23. F. Garlock, *The Big Beat*
24. *The Guardian*, 28.12.82
25. As above
26. M. Schoen, *The Psychology of Music*
27. C. Girard, *Solid Rock?*
28. Quoted in *Solid Rock?*
29. V. Wright, *Evangelism Today*, Dec. '81
30. W. Shafer, *Rock Music*
31. F. Garlock, *The Big Beat*
32. J. Fischer, *Solid Rock?*
33. As above
34. R. Taylor, *A Return to Christian Culture*
35. F. Schaeffer, *Addicted to Mediocrity*
36. E. Wright, *Tell the World*
37. J. Packer, *What is Evangelism? Theological Perspectives of Church Growth*

Chapter 7

1. Quoted in *Banner of Truth*, Jan. '77
2. As above
3. Quoted by R. Bainton, *Here I Stand*
4. *Banner of Truth*, Jan. '77
5. E. Routley, *Church Music and the Christian Faith*
6. D. Kidner, *Christian Graduate*, Mar. '81

7. A. Barnes, *Barnes' Notes on the New Testament*

Chapter 8
1. *Buzz*, Sept. '81
2. *Buzz*, Dec. '81
3. As above
4. As above
5. *Buzz*
6. *Strait*, No. 2
7. As above
8. B. Larson, *Rock and the Church*
9. *Buzz*, Sept. '82
10. K. Green, *Can God use Rock Music?*
11. A. Redpath, *Blessings out of Buffetings*
12. Quoted in *Solid Rock?*
13. *Cassells Twentieth Century Dictionary*
14. As above
15. P. Bassett, *God's Way*
16. Quoted in *D. Martyn Lloyd-Jones: The First Forty Years*
17. *Buzz*, May '81
18. As above
19. D. Porter, *Media*
20. A. Tozer, *The Divine Conquest*
21. A. Tozer, *Of God and Men*
22. *Evangelical Times*, May '79
23. J. Sidlow Baxter, *Re-thinking our Priorities*
24. E. Routley, *Church Music and the Christian Faith*
25. S. Henderson, *Whose Idea of Fun is a Nightmare?*
26. *Time*, 25.4.69
27. *Melody Maker*, 10.2.68
28. Quoted by B. Larson, *Rock and the Church*
29. G. Lees, *High Fidelity*, Feb. '70
30. I. Gitler, *Bell Telephone Magazine*, Jan.–Feb. '70
31. *Evangelical Times*, April '75
32. As above
33. *Buzz*, May '81

Chapter 9
1. J. Calvin, *Institutes, Vol. 2*
2. Augustine, *Confessions*
3. *Background to the Task*
4. *Matthew Henry's Commentary*
5. D. Wilkerson, *Get your hands off my throat*
6. Roy Connolly, *Anatomy of Pop*
7. *Reformation Today*, Nov.-Dec. '82
8. As above
9. W. Freel, *Survival?*

Chapter 10
1. B. Edwards, *Nothing but the Truth*
2. As above
3. G. Wilson, *Romans*
4. P. Bassett, *God's Way*
5. *Evangelical Times*, May '79
6. As above
7. M. Green, *Evangelism—Now and Then*
8. *Towards the Conversion of England*